FOREWORD BY
RAY BAKKE AND RICK WARREN

NEVER ALONE

From Ethiopian Villager to Global Leader

BEKELE SHANKO

·

If you have comments or questions about this book,
please contact BekeleNeverAlone@gmail.com.

Never Alone
From Ethiopian Villager to Global Leader

©2021 Bekele Shanko

Published 2021 by Global Church Movements, Orlando, FL

Cover Design: Mike Thacker

Cover Photo of Hambaricho Mounain: Courtesy of the Hambaricho Tourism and Green Development Program

print ISBN: 978-1-09839-455-4

WHAT OTHERS ARE SAYING ABOUT . . .
NEVER ALONE

Reading Bekele Shanko's story is like reading the Book of Acts. Bekele is a global visionary like few I have known. God is using Bekele to inspire the rest of us to prioritize the Great Commission. If you're wanting to live a life that causes the angels in heaven to burst into a frenzy of rejoicing, you've picked up the right book!

> DAVID NELMS, founder and president, The Timothy Initiative

As you read this story, may your heart be stirred again to believe God for the impossible personally, and also to believe this is the hour God is moving so that all may hear and have the opportunity to know Jesus Christ as Lord. Thank you, my friend, for sharing your heart, your words, your faith and your leadership.

> JIMMY SEIBERT, senior leader, Antioch Movement; senior pastor, Antioch Community Church, Waco, Texas

Never Alone is a powerful testimony of God using someone from a seemingly obscure place to help his bride, the church, grow. Flipping the cultural script from "me" to "we," Dr. Bekele Shanko's story of God's faithfulness gives clear evidence that intentional collaboration is mightily effective in advancing his kingdom and bringing glory to our triune God.

> NATE VANDER STELT, executive vice president, GACX (a global alliance for church multiplication)

The dynamics of special providence is only understood backward. If you need to supplement the global story of God who prepares His servants in unpredictable ways and invisible places, you will find strength in reading *Never Alone*.

> RAMESH RICHARD (Th.D., Ph.D.), president, RREACH; professor, Dallas Theological Seminary

Bekele Shanko is an extraordinary person. As you read his story, you may be amazed he even lived through his childhood. But, for sure, you will be amazed at how God has used him in absolutely supernatural ways. It is a great privilege for me to serve the Lord with Bekele.

> STEVE DOUGLASS, former president, Campus Crusade for Christ (known as Cru in the U.S.A.)

In the contemporary worship song "Rescue," the lyrics say: "I will send out an army to find you in the middle of darkest night. It's true, I will rescue you." We see in Dr. Bekele Shanko's story the immeasurable initiative of a Father who went to a rural African village to capture Bekele for his kingdom first and then a strategic role in the global Great Commission. And on the journey, you'll get a glimpse of his love for you.

> ROY L. PETERSON, executive coach; former president, American Bible Society

Never Alone expands our view of what's possible for the person who walks in faith and obeys the voice of the Holy Spirit. I highly recommend *Never Alone* — it will help you believe God for the impossible.

> STEPHANIE HAYES, Great Commission investor, GACX board member

Bekele Shanko grew up in a remote Ethiopian village far from civilization and the knowledge of Christ. He has become a global leader with a vision to plant five million churches. *Never Alone* tells his story. This is a book that shows how God shapes a leader and achieves His purposes in history.

> STEVE ADDISON, author, *The Rise and Fall of Movements*

Dr. Bekele offers us the story of his life — from the transformation of his family in an impoverished village of Ethiopia to his experience as a global leader — in a way that glorifies the faithfulness of God and the multiplying power of His kingdom.

DICK EASTMAN, international president, Every Home for Christ

The book shows you in a compelling way the power of partnership. You will also discover that age and experience cannot hinder visionary leaders from aiming high and achieving extraordinary results. The book also presents the role of personal effort and contribution of others in a balanced manner and with a great deal of honesty and humility. I believe the book will inspire people from all walks of life.

AKLILU DALELO WAMISHO (Ph.D.), professor of geography and environmental education, Addis Ababa University, Ethiopia

In this book, my good friend Bekele Shanko shares the supernatural way in which his family encountered God. The life transformations of his family and later on the entire village will go on to impact nations around the world. This book will remind you that God still works miracles. I recommend it highly because it will not only strengthen your faith but also enlighten you on vital lessons for being fruitful in your journey of faith.

DELANYO ADADEVOH (Ph.D.), global vice president, Campus Crusade for Christ; chairman, African Forum on Religion and Government

Reading *Never Alone* is very much like reading the Book of Acts. Luke, and now Bekele, place us at the center of church history and allow us to personally experience events that have significantly impacted Christian life.

MICHAEL WHYTE (Ph.D.), CEO and professor, Global Academy for Transformational Leadership

I have known Dr. Bekele for over three decades. We met during our undergraduate studies at Addis Ababa University in Ethiopia and share similar backgrounds. We both come from a rural region of our country, we both grew up in a family of evangelists from the Kambata people, and we both witnessed the grace of God that has brought us this far. *Never Alone* is not only a story of God's grace in Bekele's life but also describes the importance of partnerships in furthering God's kingdom. The book is a must-read for anyone considering how to make their best contributions to the kingdom of God.

TEKETEL YOHANNES ANSHEBO, former president, Ethiopian Kale Heywet Church; professor, Addis Ababa University, Ethiopia

I first met Bekele Shanko in 1997 in Geneva, Switzerland, when he attended Foundations of Personal Leadership, a course that I taught for over 25 years around the world. I have thought of Dr. Shanko as an Ethiopian Billy Graham. It has been a joy for me to journey with him as his professor and mentor.

GRACE PREEDY BARNES (Ph.D.), senior leadership consultant

Never Alone is a story of the amazing journey of an ordinary child from a physically and spiritually dark African community to a global leader! It is a living assurance of God's faithfulness and a picture of extraordinary leadership. Packed with adventures, bold steps and actions, the book uncovers the author's exceptional courage, strength, and talent to lead and operate even against the impossible. It is one of the best living examples of a true disciple of Jesus with utter submission to the Father's will and radical faith that nothing is too hard for God.

TESSEMA ERSUMO (M.D., FCS), professor of surgery, Addis Ababa University, Ethiopia

Dr. Bekele Shanko has written a compelling and transformative book. Reading it will inspire your faith in God and equip you to become a visionary leader. I have had the privilege of ministering alongside Dr. Shanko and have firsthand experience of the anointing God has on his life. His life and ministry have had a very positive effect on my life and the church that I serve. You will be glad you read this book. It will change your perspective on reaching people here, near and far!

DALE HUMMEL, senior pastor, Wooddale Church, Eden Prairie, Minnesota

A moving story of God's redemptive grace and unfailing faithfulness. It is a story of God's sovereignty and mighty work interwoven with the life of a poor and helpless child raised to play a vital role in the arena of global missional leadership. Simply remarkable and a must-read.

GIRMA BEKELE (Ph.D.), adjunct professor of missions and development studies, Wycliffe College, University of Toronto

We have a big God, so we take big risks and trust him for big results. This statement described one of our highest values at the church I led for two decades. Yet when I met Bekele, I realized that my view of God was too small. Today we work together on the GACX board trusting God for 5 million new churches among the least reached peoples of the world. I am grateful that Bekele is telling his personal story of faith, and I hope that those who read it will trust God for immeasurably more in their lives.

SCOTT RIDOUT, president, Converge

Bekele Shanko's incredible life journey serves as a model of faith in action. From a humble beginning as a boy in Ethiopia to becoming a worldwide ambassador for multiplying the harvest of souls for Jesus Christ, Bekele's story shows what one man who believes God for the impossible can accomplish. Bekele's life story should be read, studied and emulated by those who would like their lives to fulfill God's purpose in their generation.

WILLIAM S. WOJCIK, attorney at law

CONTENTS

FOREWORD BY RAY BAKKE

Ethiopia keeps on surprising me. But we should not be surprised. Ethiopia is mentioned more than 40 times in the Bible, and clearly God has gifted and chosen many for leadership both historically and in our time. I am also not surprised by Bekele Shanko's rise from a poor Ethiopian village to global leadership as a vice president of Campus Crusade for Christ and president of GACX, a global alliance for church multiplication.

As you will read in the book, Bekele established the first school in his rural village by age 13, then organized ministries that have touched thousands and thousands of people in Africa and millions around the world — all while taking time to do his doctoral studies with me and colleagues.

As someone who grew up milking cows and logging in ethnic rural America, only to be called to ministries in the largest cities of the world, I do understand that God has a sense of humor. Three words keep surfacing in Bekele's journey: vision, partnership and unity. Bekele imbibes what the late John Stott called vision: "A holy discontent with things as they are."

I wish it were in Scripture, but it's in the works of playwright George Barnard Shaw that we read: "You see things; and you say 'Why?' But I dream things that never were; and I say 'Why not?'"

We know "why." It's easier to raise the funds if we go it alone and take credit for all that happens. The truth is, however, we are never more like God, the Trinity, than when we live in community and work collaboratively in partnerships.

For me, Bekele's story became a window into holistic church planting, which points to the larger holistic end game: the kingdom.

Dr. Ray Bakke, professor of World Christian History and former chancellor at Bakke Graduate University

FOREWORD BY RICK WARREN

My friend and co-laborer Dr. Bekele Shanko is a living example of what it means to have a Great Commitment to the Great Commandment and the Great Commission. We have been friends for many years, and I have seen how his leadership is centered in Christ. Bekele has made many sacrifices in his life of commitment to Jesus.

Bekele's story *Never Alone* is full of powerful life lessons, from his childhood in a remote, non-Christian village in southern Ethiopia all the way to his current role as a global vice president of Campus Crusade for Christ (known as Cru in the United States).

He learned early and quickly many leadership lessons when serving as the Ethiopia national director for Campus Crusade in his 20s. His passion to see Ethiopia reached with the gospel, which later expanded into a vision for the entire African region, brought greater leadership learnings. Through intentionally listening to what God placed in the hearts of local, national and global leaders, as well as intentionally sharing with those he met, Bekele discovered the power and importance of collaboration.

When Bekele relocated to Campus Crusade's global headquarters in Orlando, Florida, in 2010 as a global vice president, he took this collaboration DNA with him. This is when Global Church Movements began. Bekele built on the best of what GCM/Cru had to offer and prayerfully sought collaboration opportunities with others.

God gave Bekele and his team a global vision: if one healthy, multiplying, sustainable church or faith community were to be established for every 1,000 people on planet Earth (1:1000), the world could be reached. In 2011, five ministries came together around the 1:1000 vision to form a global alliance for church multiplication, known as GACX. Today, GACX has grown to more than 100 global ministries and organizations who serve as implementers and accelerators toward seeing the vision become a reality.

In 2018, GACX and four additional church-planting networks (24:14, ETHNE, Vision 5:9 and Global Church Planting Network) began discussing the possibility of collaborating around church-planting movements that God was birthing around the world. They came to me at the annual Finishing the Task conference, shared this exciting idea and in 2019 asked me to assume leadership.

Our vision in FTT is to complete three goals, or "finish lines," by A.D. 2033, the 2,000th anniversary of the Great Commission that Jesus gave to us (if you use the Christian calendar). The goals include *Bibles* (a complete Bible in all 7,000 languages), *Believers* (the Good News continuously available to every person in a language they can understand) and *Bodies* (a church for every 1,000 people).

Did you catch the last B goal? Bekele's vision has spread throughout the church-planting movement world.

This is why I asked Bekele to lead FTT's global effort of helping to establish a church or missional community in every place and every people across the world through partnership initiatives. Bekele is not just a great leader. He has demonstrated over and over that he is a servant leader. He is a servant who leads. And partners serve each other. I could think of no better person to lead this initiative than Bekele, with his fruitful track record of leadership, servanthood and partnership. (Cru has also demonstrated this attitude of partnership in allowing Bekele to devote some of his time to FTT, while still leading GCM and GACX).

May this book guide you into biblical principles of never leading alone. God is with us, and He has designed us to be better together.

Rick Warren, founding pastor of Saddleback Church in Southern California and author of *The Purpose Driven Life*

INTRODUCTION

I love numbers. Back in college, I majored in statistics and mathematics. So one day in 2019 I asked Siri, the invisible search assistant, how many books have so far been written in the world. Her answer? A staggering 129,864,880! That number is not only stunning but also frightening. Why on earth am I adding one more book?

The answer is simple: No one has ever written, or will write, the book that I alone can write; it's about my life, what I have learned and my experiences of leadership. Since I am a unique creation with a unique journey of life, the content of my book is also unique. If I don't tell my story, no one else would and no one else could.

The book tells the story the Creator has been writing in and through my life. Apart from committing the time to remember, reflect and write, I have contributed almost nothing to the making of the story. It's all about God and his grace. Just as a good shepherd picks up a wounded lamb, God picked me up from a materially impoverished and spiritually deprived village in Ethiopia, carried me in his arms and gave me a cause to live for.

The book is not only about me but also about the uncountable men and women from past and present who have instructed, inspired and influenced me. Partnership is in my blood. As you read through the book, you will discover why. Partnership is what I have done for most of my life. That's why I chose the title *Never Alone*.

"No man is an island," said the 17th-century English poet and preacher John Donne. No person can survive in this world without receiving help from others. I have not come to this point by myself but with the help of many loving, inspiring, and generous men and women from near and far, people who have schooled, shielded, supported and strengthened me.

If you read the book carefully and reflectively, I promise you will be encouraged, motivated and challenged by the stories of faith, adventure, perseverance and triumph. You will meet me as a penniless boy in rural Ethiopia who pioneered an elementary school at age 13, as a college graduate and government worker at age 19, and as national director of a nonprofit organization at age 26. You will be intrigued by the marvelous story of redemption and destiny, spiritual laxity and renewal, divine calling and innovative leadership, and the power and practices of partnerships.

At the end of each chapter, I've included reflection questions. I would encourage you to pause and consider taking some tangible steps of action in your life and leadership before moving on to the next chapter. Much of the benefit of a book such as this comes from your reflections on the content, and your willingness to put into practice what you learn.

Who is this book for? If you are searching for God or desiring to know God's will in your life, no doubt this book can help. If you are a new leader in an organization or starting something and wondering where and how to start, you will glean important insights. If you would like to learn how to initiate, develop, and manage local, national and international partnerships with individuals and organizations, you have the right tool in your hand. If you sense God is calling you to do something bigger than yourself and you are not sure if you are the one to do it, the content of this book will energize you to take bold steps of faith.

Moreover, if you would like to know how to creatively mobilize human, financial and material resources, or design and lead complex projects, you will be glad you have the book. If you are a younger leader and want to learn how to increase your influence, the book is for you. I know what it means to be a younger leader. I have assumed new leadership positions approximately every five years of my life, starting as a young teen. You will learn from my experiences.

In Chapters 1 and 2, you will read about my testimony and the most important factors that shaped my childhood and teenage years. Chapters 3 to 6 describe my faith adventures and some of the creative ways I was involved in mobilizing people and material resources in Ethiopia. Chapters 7 and 8 highlight the development and implementation of a bold vision to saturate the city of Addis Ababa with the gospel of Jesus in 52 days. In Chapters 9 and 10, you will be inspired by the story of an evangelistic campaign to reach 50 million people in 50 cities over 50 days across 23 countries in Africa. Chapters 11 and 12 paint a picture of me standing at the crossroads wondering which way to go and how I found the right path. Chapters 13 to 16 present the global leadership challenge I was given and what has happened as a result. And in Chapter 17, I take you back to my childhood village in Ethiopia.

Finally, I have included four appendices. Please take special note of the first three: leadership lessons I have learned over the years, partnership principles that guide my actions and a crucial partnership process.

Read carefully and read all of it. Behold, I add one more book to the millions of books written thus far. But this book is one of a kind — the story of God's grace, the impact of many people in my life and how a merciful God can use the most unlikely person to fulfill his eternal purpose. Behold, I present to you the story of God's favor in my life. Enjoy! If you have a question or comment, please write to me at BekeleNeverAlone@gmail.com.

CHAPTER 1

My Redemption Story

"The thief comes only to steal and kill and destroy;
I have come that they may have life, and have it
to the full" (John 10:10)

Let me take you on a journey to a remote village in south central Ethiopia. . . .

Welcome to a place far from civilization and stricken by abject material poverty. No electricity, no tap water, no church, no health facility. This is where I was born, in a small village on the outskirts of the town of Angacha. In medical emergencies or life-threatening situations, the whole community would come together and care for the sick.

When the ill needed more medical attention than the community could give, four strong men would place the sick person on an improvised stretcher, then carry it on their shoulders to Wasera, a Catholic mission health center about 10 miles away.

Nothing would stop them — not the scorching heat of summer, not the slippery mud of winter, not the darkest hours of night. Yet with hills to climb, valleys to descend and rivers to cross, the journey took three to four hours on foot; and only the fortunate ones made it to the health center and received treatment. Others died on the way.

Malaria and infectious diseases ran rampant. Preventable diseases cut short many precious lives. Spiritual darkness covered hundreds of villages. Many believed in a supreme being that existed somewhere in the skies, but no one knew for sure if the deity were accessible by ordinary people. People hoped to gain access to the supreme being through witch doctors and "sacred" agents such as rocks, rivers, big trees, the sun or the moon.

My father feared and served a tribal spiritual leader who possessed a "divine" power to control nature. The leader, known as Abba-Sarecho (who also happened to be a distant cousin), was regarded as a nobleman with a discerning spirit. He commanded the rains to come or to stop, the harvest to wither, or one tribe to defeat another tribe in battle. In effect, he was king of our small community; and we were his subjects, living in fear and hopelessness.

People from distant places flooded the king's residential compound (which was considered holy ground), bringing gifts such as cattle, grain or money, and seeking solutions to their problems. They wanted power to defeat their enemies, the ability to bear children or simply greater wealth.

Isolated from the rest of the communities, the king lived on a hilltop of Hambaricho Mountain. No one dared to lift their heads in his presence, look at his face or call him a witch doctor. People usually bowed before him and waited for him to pronounce judgment — curses or blessings — depending on the issue at hand. He usually wore white robes and was regarded as a mediator between heaven and earth. People feared him and trembled at his presence, and subjects who failed to fulfill his requirements were attacked by evil spirits.

Abba-Sarecho usually gave his followers specific instructions. For instance, my father was required to drink *araki* (an Ethiopian hard liquor) and smoke tobacco. Often, when under that influence, my father would verbally abuse as well as hit his wives. On holidays and special occasions when food was prepared, my father would take the first portion of the food and place it under an old coffee tree behind our house, hoping to bring pleasure to the spiritual powers and peace to our family.

If the powers were happy, then the food would disappear, meaning my father's sacrifice was accepted. But if the food remained under the tree for hours, then it meant the spiritual authorities were unhappy with my father, which would prompt him to beg for mercy. But mercy was not easily found.

In search of mercy and hope, my father would sacrifice a chicken or a lamb. As a poor farmer, my father owned little — a few cows for milk, a pair of oxen to plow our small farm, some sheep and a few chickens. We ate meat only during holidays or when my father earned some extra money.

My father was one of the millions of Ethiopians exploited by feudal landlords until the latter were stripped of their status and privileges during the Ethiopian communist revolution of 1974-91. When the revolution began, people hoped it would help solve the nation's socioeconomic problems. In reality, however, the government used Marxist ideology to take control of private institutions and properties and centralize nearly everything. The communist regime kept the country under its grip for 17 years, destroying the socioeconomic, cultural and religious fabric of our society.

Because my father earned too small an income to sustain the family, he often traveled to distant regions of the country searching for jobs as a day laborer. Despite the meager wages, he would leave his family for weeks or months at a time, doing all he could to put food on the table and save a bit of money for social obligations, government taxes and emergencies. But most of the time we were penniless. I will never forget the feeling of hopelessness and the impact of poverty I felt on a particular Tuesday afternoon.

I Hate Poverty

I was in middle school and attending seventh grade. Tuesday was a special day of the week. There was, and still is, a popular public market known as the Angacha market, where almost everybody and everything in the community came together. This included people, animals, dairy products, meat, fresh vegetables, food, drinks, and used and new clothing.

People walked for hours to get to the market. Most went to exchange goods, but some went to socialize, engage in cultural and political discussions, meet relatives and friends, and eat and drink together.

Market day generated great excitement for us as students. We would get out of school early, then look for our parents at the market and insist that they buy us something. As kids, we always thought we had the right to get anything we wanted from our parents. For whatever reason, parents who could not buy things for their children on Tuesdays were the subject of gossip and grumbling among the students on Wednesdays.

One particular Tuesday, I was happy to find my father in the market. I wanted him to buy me a stick of sugarcane, which would probably cost about 5 cents. But he told me he had no money. Full of anger and disappointment, I left my father in the market and walked home crying.

The 30-minute walk home felt like an eternity. My father's heart was broken because he could not afford to give 5 cents to his son. Thus, whenever he walked me to school, he would encourage me to keep my focus on education so that I would not be poor like him.

Polygamy was a common practice in those villages before the introduction of the gospel, and my father had three wives who bore him 18 children. Whenever my father failed to satisfy the demands of the evil spirits, our family was severely punished in mysterious ways. Over the years, four children from each wife would die — that is, 12 out of his 18 children.

A few years ago, I had an opportunity to visit my birthplace. I asked my uncle Abebe Shamebo to tell me more about our family's past. He told me that after losing the first seven or eight children, my father was so devastated and ashamed that he would not even let his brothers know that another child had died. Instead, he would bury the dead by himself.

After all four children from his first wife had died, my father was under pressure from the family and the community to divorce her. This was a norm in the community. A barren wife, or one whose child had died, was considered disgraceful or cursed.

My mother was my father's second wife. She gave birth to nine children, of whom only five survived. My father inherited his third wife when his uncle died and he was expected to marry the widow, just as in the old Hebrew tradition. Of my father's five children with her, only one survived.

People in Western societies may not understand the work of evil spirits, but those forces of darkness hit our family hard. Pain and sorrow shadowed us. It seemed we were destined for despair and thus lived under great fear and hopelessness.

In fact, my parents did not even give me a name for several years because they were afraid I might also die like my siblings. But at age 4 I received my name, Bekele (beh-KEH-leh) — an Ethiopian Amharic name meaning "germinated" or "sprouted." The name signifies life, hope and victory. It was a prophetic name, indicating the great victory the Creator of the universe would grant us a year later.

From my beginnings in the fear, spiritual darkness and poverty of an Ethiopian village, God would radically change my life. And he did so through an amazing partnership of heaven and earth, angels and men, the divine and the ordinary. I would come to see that "partnership dance" as God's signature in my life, and it became my mission to open others' eyes to see it as well.

At the Gates of Heaven and Hell

When I was 5, my father told us he was having some strange visions. He described how, over the previous five years, an angel of the Lord had visited him once a year in a dream. But when I was 5 years old, instead of just one angel, two angels clothed in bright white appeared to him at night, sat next to his bed and taught him about God. One of the angels carried a large sword.

After the angels had taught him for hours that night, they took him to heaven and gave him a tour of heaven and hell. The angels stopped him at the gates of hell, where he faced a deep darkness and heard the loud screams of terrified people. I can't explain to you how my father was taken to heaven, but it happened to him. For my father, heaven and hell are real. He walked on the streets of heaven and stood at the gates of hell.

With great emotion, my father explained his experience of those places. He said heaven is a place of beauty, perfection and peace while hell is a terrible place. After his tour of heaven and hell, one of the angels asked my father, "Now that I have shown you two different places, which one do you choose?"

"Please let me stay in heaven!" my father cried out. "Don't send me to hell."

The angel smiled and said, "You have made the right choice. I will send you two men who will come to your home and tell you how you can get into heaven. Then you must listen and do what they tell you to do. But if you reject their message, I will cut you into pieces by this sword."

A few days later, God sent two men from a neighboring village to show my father the way to heaven. The men were illiterate farmers who had become followers of Christ just a week or so earlier. The God of mercy appeared and instructed them to go and tell my father that the only way he could enter heaven was by denying the evil spirits and believing in Jesus.

The men explained that Jesus is the Son of God who came down from heaven to die on the cross for the sins of mankind; that God has offered forgiveness of sins and salvation for all who believe in the name of Jesus. The men invited my father to deny demons and believe in Jesus. If he were to believe in Jesus, the men explained, then my father would receive peace and eternal life, he would stop smoking and drinking, he would give dignity to his wives, and he would become the husband of one wife. Later it became a common practice for a husband of multiple wives to choose one wife after becoming a Christian. The Christian community would then take care of the other women, farming and harvesting their land.

That evening the two men shared with us the greatest news ever told to humanity: salvation and hope in Jesus Christ. I remember vividly that I was sitting on the floor with my older sister while my parents sat on chairs. I stood up, walked to the two men and asked, "Would my dad stop beating my mom if he believed in Jesus?"

"Yes," they answered.

Though at age 5 I did not fully understand what it meant to believe in Jesus, I was the first person in my family to do so. I was desperate to have peace in our family and to give dignity to my mother.

The men asked me to raise my right hand as a sign of surrendering my life to God and led me to believe in Jesus through repeating a short and simple prayer: "I deny evil spirits; I believe in Jesus."

Immediately after that short confession, I was born again into the eternal family of God and became a follower of Jesus. It was a defining moment in my life, and I would never be the same. Through the work of the Holy Spirit, I was instantly transferred from the kingdom of darkness into the kingdom of light. My parents and my older sister also prayed the same prayer that night.

I am amazed to think that although the angels could have told my father how he could enter heaven, they did not. Instead, they transferred the responsibility of telling the good news to two ordinary men. Why? Because God fulfills his plans through people who are willing to be used by him. Though God could fulfill his plan without us, he chooses to include us.

On that blessed evening, God enabled my parents and my sister and I to reject despair and death and choose hope and life. A supernatural light from heaven penetrated our darkness. By accepting the gospel, we crossed from hell to heaven, from darkness to light, and from oppression to freedom. We received a crown of beauty instead of ashes, joy instead of mourning and praise instead of despair.[1]

The good news that the prophet Isaiah heralded to the Israelites suddenly became real to us: "The people walking in darkness have seen a great light; on those living in the land of deep darkness a light has dawned."[2] Indeed, the bright light from heaven overcame the deepest darkness of our life and our village. We became Christians, followers of Jesus Christ.

A couple of years after that night in our humble village, my father decided to keep my mother as his chosen wife while our church took the responsibility of caring for his third wife until she died about 10 years later.[3] Also, I started preschool a few months after we became Christians. New life, new journey, new destiny! Moreover, all five of the children born to my parents after we became Christians are still alive today. We truly experienced what Jesus promised, "The thief comes only to steal and kill and destroy; I have come that they may have life, and have it to the full."[4]

My Father's Miracle

My father had never been to school, so he was unable to read or write. A few days after we became believers in Christ, my father experienced another miracle. As he was tending cows alongside a river, he found a Bible lying on the ground. We don't know how that Bible ended up in that particular location in a remote village. But my father picked it up and started flipping through the pages. Suddenly he heard a voice saying, "This is my Word." He did not know who was speaking to him, as there was no human being nearby. Then he felt as though somebody was telling him to sit down under the shade of a nearby tree.

He found the shade, sat down and prayed something like, "Lord, was that your voice? Is this your Word? You know that I can't read. Would you help me read this book?"

Without really knowing what he was saying, my father promised God, "If you enable me to read this book, I will teach this book to many people and do so for the rest of my life."

I believe it was the Holy Spirit who inspired my father to pray like that. Right there, alongside a river in a remote Ethiopian village, the Almighty God gave my father a supernatural ability to read. And my father started teaching the Bible that very day. He invited villagers to come to our home, where he shared his story and told all that had happened to him over the past few days.

Indeed, many things had happened. The angels, the tour of heaven and hell, the two men, discovering the way to heaven, the Bible on the ground, a voice from heaven, his prayer, and the ability to read the Bible. Instantly, there was a new evangelist in the area. He read the Bible to the crowd gathered in front of our house, then boldly invited them to reject the worship of evil spirits and the many unknown gods and turn to the Creator God through Jesus Christ.

That evening, in the bright moonlight in front of our primitive dwelling place, the grace and the glory of God covered the residents. God brought the entire village into his kingdom.[5]

God enabled my father to fulfill his promise to teach the Bible until the end of his life. He proclaimed the gospel to many people for the next 37 years until his Master took him to glory on January 18, 2011, at age 84.

One of the greatest miracles was seeing that my father could read the Bible for all those years but not any other book. Other books had the same Amharic script as the Bible, yet he could not read them.

God used my father to bring many people into his kingdom. He traveled through many villages casting out demons, preaching the gospel of freedom and sharing the joy of God's grace with other believers. A few days before he left this earth, he asked the family to inscribe the words of the apostle Paul on his tombstone: "I have fought the good fight, I have finished the race, I have kept the faith."[6]

We serve an almighty God. Nothing is too hard for him.

It Is Not Good

Why am I telling you about my salvation story in a book about partnerships? I have a reason. Partnerships start in our heart, soul and mind. Partnerships are meaningless unless our ministries are deeply rooted in our redemption story. Reflecting on God's story in our own life, and remembering the countless people who have shaped us, inspires us to understand and practice partnerships.

As a person and leader, I am a product of partnerships. Physically, I came into this world through the partnership of my parents, through their union in marriage. Spiritually, I am a product of many people and circumstances.

Indeed, heaven and earth partnered in my redemption. God the Father sent his Son to die on the cross for me. Jesus sent those angels to visit. The Holy Spirit inspired two illiterate farmers to tell us the good news. Some generous people — probably in North America or Europe or Australia — funded the translation, printing and distribution of Bibles in Ethiopia such that my father might find one of those Bibles lying on the ground. I am sure there were also many believers near and far faithfully praying for the gospel to be preached among those who had never heard, including my village.

Then the Holy Spirit opened our hearts to accept the good news.

Can you imagine how many people, families, agencies, churches, donors and angels have partnered in my redemption story? I am greatly indebted to all of them. How about you? How was your redemption story written? How many people have participated in your salvation?

You are a product of partnerships. You came to this world through partnerships; you were saved because of partnerships. Whether you realize it or not, you are protected and cared for through partnerships. You are not here by yourself, but rather have been shaped by countless people, various circumstances and God himself.

When I teach a leadership class on partnerships, I ask my students not to eat any food unless they were fully responsible for preparing the meals. In other words, they could not eat if any other person had contributed to the process of creating the meal.

Let me challenge you in the same way. Suppose you wanted to fix your own breakfast: an omelet, slices of toasted bread, a glass of fresh orange juice and a freshly brewed cup of Ethiopian coffee. And you don't want help from anybody. That means you must own and raise your own chicken; grow your own tomatoes, onions and green peppers; manufacture your own stove, oven or toaster; create and supply your own electricity, gas or fire; plant, grow and harvest your own Ethiopian coffee; and the list goes on and on.

Without other people, life is not only meaningless but also impossible. We live because of others and through partnerships. But we often fail to recognize the enormous benefits we receive from other people.

May I suggest that you take a moment right now and think about the people who have made significant contributions in your life? Start by listing their names, then writing down at least one major contribution each person has made. Take action to in some way thank these individuals for what they have done for you.

It is not surprising that even God realized the value of partnership. After evaluating the works of his creation, God concluded, "It is not good for the man to be alone."[7] Hence, God decided to create a helper just right for him. Yes, a helper — a collaborator, coworker, colleague and partner.

I believe God did some experiments to see what life would be like without partnership. Then he concluded, "It is not good."

There are billions of people waiting to hear the life-changing message of our Lord Jesus Christ. There are millions of Bekeles out there in the world, broken and hopeless, waiting for somebody to intercede for their salvation, for somebody to go and proclaim the good news, for somebody to fund a Bible translation or distribution, for somebody to help train a local believer, or for somebody to help plant a church.

What if we who are transformed by the power of the gospel of Jesus were united and working together to make Jesus known in the whole world? What if the world could see the depth of God's grace, the power of brotherly love, and the practice of partnerships in and through us?

I came into this world because of partnerships. My redemption story was possible because of partnerships. My village was transformed by the power of the gospel because of partnerships. There were various types of partnerships in my redemption story: heaven and earth, divine and ordinary, people from near and far.

Partnership is not only what can happen to you because of other people, but also what can happen to others because of you. Partnerships have shaped not only my story of redemption in significant ways but also my formative years.

Questions for personal and group reflection

1. What have you learned from Bekele's life story about the power of the gospel in transforming a person's life?

2. What is your salvation story? How has the gospel of Jesus Christ transformed your life?

3. What other partnerships have had a significant impact on your life and ministry?

4. Please respond: *One way I will take action to appreciate someone who has had a significant impact on my life is* _____

_____

_____

_____

A typical rural home in southern Ethiopia

Bekele's dad, Shanko Mamiru, holding his Bible

Tachigna Angacha Elementary School — the school Bekele founded at age 13

CHAPTER 2

My Formative Years

"It takes a village to raise a child"
— Igbo and Yoruba proverb

In my development as a leader, I've found it crucial to reflect on my life's journey and remember critical steps along the way. I enjoy taking time to remember people who have contributed to my development: family and friends, teachers and authors, young and old, educated and uneducated, pastors and preachers, people from past and present and near and far. Some influenced me directly, others indirectly; some actively, others passively. Their influence, whether meant for good or evil, has brought vitality and strength to my life. In fact, I would say that my greatest learning experiences have taken place during the most challenging circumstances.

I am not here by accident. You may think you are solely responsible for the path you have taken so far in life and for who you are today. But I hope you realize that many people and circumstances have directly and indirectly shaped your life. Whether you recognize them or not, the visible and invisible fingerprints of many people are all over you.

It would be impossible to mention all the people and circumstances that have influenced my own life during my formative years, but let me highlight a few.

My Parents: Fighting Illiteracy

Unlike many kids in my village, I was given the rare opportunity to be educated. Most kids in my village, with whom I tended sheep or played street soccer, did not even complete high school. Many died of preventable diseases due to a lack of basic medical services.

My parents played a key role in my development. They lacked material resources but worked hard to provide me with food, clothing and school supplies. Kerosene light or fireside flames were our only options for light, so my mother bought kerosene for me to do my homework at night. I have tasted the bitterness of poverty.

I did not get my first pair of shoes until ninth grade, which I bought myself with money I'd earned by teaching students in a school I had established when I was 13. Later it became a public school that is still functioning in my village. Thanks to my parents who had a vision for my future, I overcame illiteracy and poverty.

During my preschool and early elementary school years, my mother bought books by selling firewood and homemade cheese at local markets. And both of my parents allowed me to focus on reading instead of tending cattle and working on the farm. "I don't want you to be illiterate like me," my father always said. "Your mother and I want a better future for you."

Though uneducated, my father knew the value of education. He continuously encouraged me to read books, complete my homework and excel in academic performance. By the grace of God and through the constant prayer and support of my parents, I became one of the best students in the school.

My Village: Enfolding Me

According to an ancient African proverb, it takes the whole community to raise a child. In my village, most of the parents were responsible for all the children. In those days, and still today to some extent, almost any adult person in the community had the right to discipline anybody's child who did something wrong.

Parents whose children were disciplined by others were expected to thank those who took care of their children.

No person would go hungry in our community, because we believed, "What is yours is mine, and what is mine is yours." Such practice was not meant to encourage laziness or dependence, but rather promote love, care and generosity. The community would, in fact, shame a person who was lazy, selfish or greedy. This partnership between persons was one of the guiding principles in our community.

Every family in our community had a piece of farmland. We harvested a little bit of everything: corn, wheat, beans, bananas, potatoes, sugarcane and teff (an Ethiopian grain and the staple of our diet). When I was 7 years old, I began helping my father on the farm. Child labor was never an issue. Boys helped fathers on the farms while girls helped mothers at home. Our fathers taught us to assume responsibility from an early age. Every male child was given a small portion of land to cultivate, where he could learn about productivity.

As children, we knew that we would complete our individual tasks faster if we worked together with other kids. So, three to seven kids would form a group and work together. We would go from farm to farm, working and eating together. The family for whom we worked provided food. Our parents visited our small farm plots, appreciating the good work and helping us learn from our mistakes. They instilled in us the practices of mentoring.

We children also learned about life as we played together, ate together and assumed responsibilities. Partnership was not something abstract or extra but a means of survival and an integral part of life.

Years later that caring community would again enfold me each time I visited during breaks from college. When I arrived, my parents and siblings, aunts and uncles, and cousins and nephews would gather to welcome me with laughter, food and coffee. And when it was time to head back to school, they'd gather once again, even contributing money toward my transportation and school supplies.

Over the intervening years, I completed grades two, three and four in a single year, becoming the youngest student in my high-school class. And because

I was also the best student in the class, I often served as a substitute teacher. The school principal, as well as my classmates, approved my role, but that required me to study the textbooks ahead of my classmates.

My accomplishments in high school, however, along with the immaturity of my teenage brain, led me to pride, independence and rebellion. I stopped going to church and refused to meet with believers, especially those who encouraged me to maintain my spirituality. I believed that students with poor academic performances needed God's help, but not me. Instead, I surrounded myself with those who didn't believe in Jesus and no longer went to church.

This went on for two years. Although I didn't have material resources to squander, like the prodigal son described in Luke 15, I was in a spiritual wilderness during the last two years of high school. I lost my fellowship with God, the joy of going to church with my family and the privilege of singing in a youth choir.

Nevertheless, my father was quietly and faithfully praying for me, asking God to intervene in my life. Indeed, God intervened in a dramatic way. After completing high school, the time came to leave my village. At age 16, for the first time in my life, I was on a public bus traveling to the capital city for a university education.

With 62 passengers and every seat occupied, the bus traveled in slow motion toward the city and Addis Ababa University. The 150-mile trip took six or seven hours on those rough and dusty roads, giving me time for self-reflection. As my brain scanned through the unwritten pages of my life, suddenly I became overwhelmed by the goodness of God. It seemed so strange that out of 269 students who took the national examination with me at Angacha High School in the 1983-84 academic year, I was the only student who qualified to go to university.

Community leaders had started the high school so that youth from our area wouldn't have to walk for hours to the nearest school, about 20 miles away. As a higher grade was added each year, the same teachers were promoted to teach it — some of whom didn't even have a bachelor's degree. For example, when grade

10 was opened, we had the same teachers who had taught us in grade 9. My class was the first cohort of students to attend grade 12.

The school was built with sticks, mud, straw and corrugated iron, with a dirt floor. The library didn't have books, so I borrowed notes from friends who attended high school elsewhere. For me, to pass the national examination and go to college was an absolute favor from God.

In those days, with only two universities in Ethiopia — Addis Ababa University and Asmara University[8] — most students who completed high school had few opportunities to go to college. As we continued our bus ride to Addis Ababa, many questions troubled me: "Why me?" "What about the other students who didn't pass the examination?" "What would their future be like?" "What good have I done to deserve this?"

A sense of fear, guilt and emptiness inundated my heart. Suddenly I heard a voice, *Behold, I have engraved you on the palms of my hands; your walls are ever before me.*[9] I didn't know God was speaking to me. I thought everybody on the bus heard the voice, but to my surprise no one did.

It was only a few months later that I realized God had spoken those same words through the prophet Isaiah when the Israelites were captives in Babylonia. Likewise, I was in a spiritual captivity and the walls of my life were in ruins. But God had his eye on me, even in that public bus on that dusty road, and even when I didn't recognize his voice. The love of God always amazes me. He reaches down into our lowest points of brokenness to lift us up and lift us high.

I arrived in the capital city and completed the registration process. One sunny afternoon in September, when the spring flowers were beginning to bloom, I was taking a walk around the campus when a senior student approached me.

"Can I talk to you for a moment?" he asked.

"Yes." I replied.

"Do you know Jesus?"

"I used to know him, but not now."

"Would you tell me what happened?"

"I can't tell you!" I shot back, proud and arrogant.

"Do you have a Bible?" he responded, full of patience and love.

When I told him I didn't have one, he offered me a small New Testament published by The Gideons International. I accepted reluctantly. He then invited me to join a group of students who met at 5 p.m. on Wednesdays to study the Bible.

I ended the conversation by telling him I would think about his offer, and we went our separate ways. For the next three days, I considered rejecting the student's invitation. But God was at work, and at 5 p.m. Wednesday I showed up in room 301 of Asfawosen Building.[10]

Room 301: God Calling Me

After spending an hour with six students studying the Bible, I was stunned. They were different from Christians I had known before. They were not following a Christian religion but rather had a vital and contagious relationship with Jesus and were filled with the joy of the Holy Spirit. All of a sudden, Jesus became real to me.

Through that one-hour encounter with both the students and the Word of God, I was confronted with a reality I couldn't reject: I must completely surrender my life to Jesus or walk away in denial. At the end of the study, everyone left the room except me and the group leader — who stayed because it was his dorm. But I stayed because God was calling me to surrender my life to Jesus.

Room 301 seemed to me like the Mount of Transfiguration, where Peter wanted to make three huts — one for Jesus, one for Moses and one for Elijah — and stay there. Asfaw Keno, the group leader, asked if I needed any help. I was feeling a sense of guilt and shame. My heart was beating faster. It was my first real encounter with the Holy Spirit. For the first time in my life, I understood the Person and the power of the Holy Spirit. I told Asfaw I wanted to be like him and the other students in the group.

Overwhelmed by the presence of the Holy Spirit in the room, I knelt for the first time in two years and rededicated my life to the risen Christ. In that small room with a bunk bed and just enough space to hold two chairs and a small study desk, the Creator of the universe started the work of transformation in my life. My relationship with Jesus was restored and a heavenly fire began to burn within me. I left the room a new person, full of joy and peace.

For the next four years, I grew in my spiritual life and leadership responsibilities. I moved from being a Bible study group member to a group leader and then part of the campus ministry leadership team. While at Addis Ababa University, I received training from the organization that sponsored our groups: the Great Commission Ministry of Ethiopia (a ministry of Campus Crusade for Christ International).[11] That training sparked a vision in me and a love for people without Christ. For the first time, I understood that every Christian has an obligation to introduce people to Jesus.

A Hostile Environment: Preparing Me

The four years of campus ministry laid a strong foundation for my spiritual, mental and leadership development. During that time, and even during my high-school years,[12] the Marxist ideology of the Soviet Union was ravishing our country.[13] The communist government was completely against God. The political cadres tried to force us to chant slogans such as, "There is no God," "Revolution above everything," "Ethiopia first," and "Down with capitalism." But as followers of Christ, we refused to comply. We were willing to die for our faith in Jesus.

Most churches were shut down. The government took possession of Christian mission stations, church properties, and private hospitals and schools. Religious institutions and social service centers were converted into government offices, while storage rooms and meeting halls were used to study the works of Marx, Lenin and Engels. As Christian students, we were continuously harassed, arrested and interrogated. But by the grace of God, we stood firm in our faith.

On the university campus, particularly at the Faculty of Natural Science, 88 of us were blacklisted as "anti-socialists and followers of imported religion" just because we believed in Christ. We were repeatedly warned that if one more person converted to Christianity, we would be dismissed from campus. Activities like carrying the Bible, praying in the cafeteria, meeting with believers or telling other students about Jesus became illegal. However, the Holy Spirit was moving so powerfully on our campus that just as in the Book of Acts, God was daily adding those who believed in Jesus.

Being a follower of Christ was such a precious thing that our commitment to Jesus was very high. There were only two options: You were a fully committed Christian or you were not a Christian at all. There was no middle ground, no compromise, no lukewarm Christianity. Choosing to be a Christian meant choosing rejection, persecution or even death. True Christians were not afraid of death, which we considered to be a shortcut to be united with our heavenly Father forever. We told our persecutors, "If you kill us, you would be sending us to heaven. But we don't want to go to heaven without you because Jesus also died for you."

Prayer was our secret weapon. Whenever threatened, we would secretly gather in someone's house and pray through the night. We cherished prayers, loved the Word of God and grew spiritually through small-group Bible studies. We discovered that essential strategies for the growth of the underground church included fervent prayer, evangelistic Bible studies, and the intentional development and multiplication of small-group leaders.

During those years of hardship, we received lots of encouragement from Christians around the world. Christian literature was smuggled into the country and landed in our hands. We treasured and devoured material such as *Decision* magazine by the Billy Graham Evangelistic Association; updates from Dr. David Yonggi Cho of the Yoido Full Gospel Church in Seoul, Korea; *The Herald of His Coming* newspaper from Gospel Revivals Inc.; and handwritten letters from Mother Basilea Schlink, leader of the Evangelical Sisterhood of Mary in Darmstadt, Germany.

Mother Basilea's letters, translated and printed in Amharic, were like hot soup from heaven. We loved every word she wrote. We circulated those messages among believers inside and outside the university campus. Though we wanted to keep those materials to ourselves and read them again and again, we could not keep them because of the spiritual hunger around us. Whoever wanted to keep the content was required to copy them by hand and store them in a safe place, otherwise the secret police would confiscate the materials and put us in jail.

Moreover, books such as *Tortured for Christ* and *The Pilgrim's Progress* gave us courage, encouragement and hope. Persecution was like fuel added to a blazing spiritual fire. It stoked our passion for the Lord and for his eternal kingdom. Some of the finest Ethiopian spiritual leaders of our generation emerged through that persecution. And God did many miracles.

My Wife: The Best Partner

Long ago King Solomon concluded, "He who finds a wife finds what is good and receives favor from the Lord."[14] So at age 17 and as a sophomore in college, I went to attend a marriage seminar organized for a class of graduating seniors. However, the seniors stopped me at the entrance and said, "Brother, you are too young for this. Go back." They sent me back and I was disappointed.

Then I thought of teaching myself about marriage. I looked for books to read. One of the books that made a great impact on me was *Do All to the Glory of God* by Watchman Nee. It may not be considered a book on marriage, but it was insightful. The author offers a few chapters on family, including mating, marriage and parenting. I gleaned important tips on how to choose a marriage partner.

One of those tips was the importance of spiritual and mental preparation to receive my future wife. One statement in particular made a lasting impression: "A Christian can jump into marriage but he cannot jump out of it. We Christians cannot behave like people in the world who easily marry and easily divorce. We cannot jump out. Therefore, before you jump in, consider carefully."[15]

The author further explains that a Christian marriage is not an experiment but a covenant relationship, not a contract but a lifetime commitment, and not selfish but sacrificial. He suggests to readers who desire to be married that they develop a habit of daily praying for and blessing their future spouses in the name of the Lord.

Inspired by the reading, I started a journey of blessing my future wife without even knowing who she was. I often blessed her, our children, grandchildren and our future generations. I asked God to prepare me to be the right fit for my wife. After praying for about seven years, I met the girl God had prepared for me.

She attended the same local church as me. Since almost all evangelical churches in the city had been shut down by the communist government, believers from other congregations came to worship at our church. Fortunately, though threatened many times, our local church was not closed by the communists. Perhaps our church stayed open because we had an excellent elementary and middle school, to which even the politicians were sending their children. With three services on Sundays, the church was crowded, and it was almost impossible to know everyone personally.

Shewa and I met in March 1991. The very first day I saw her, I knew she was the one for me. We became friends, started praying together and grew in our relationship. Since we lived in the same city, we talked to each other daily. Spiritual conversations and prayer were at the core of our growing relationship. Every time we met, we shared with one another what God was teaching us through his Word, and we prayed together.

Mutual friends prayed for, encouraged and supported us on our journey.[16] As our relationship grew, we informed our local church with a written letter about our intention for engagement and marriage. The elders invited us for an interview. We explained how we met and how we knew it was God's will for us to be married. We passed the interview, and the elders assigned people who provided premarital counseling.

We got married on August 19, 1992, and now we have four wonderful children, two boys and two girls: Nathan, Elim, Philip and Nesiel.

Shewa is a perfect fit for me; her strengths and gifts complement me. She is an extrovert who is energized by being with people, while I am an introvert who loves a quiet environment. She is driven by love and care for people, while I am driven by getting things done.

I am a rural boy and she is a city girl. She always reminds me how important it is to maintain my friends, balance my priorities, spend quality time with our children, cultivate my spiritual disciplines and take good care of people who work with me. She is extremely compassionate, generous and discerning. For nearly three decades now, she has been faithfully serving the Lord, our family, friends, staff and the people around us with passion and compassion.

In 1993, Shewa and I joined the Great Commission Ministry of Ethiopia and moved to Kampala, Uganda, for new staff training. We would stay there for almost a year, during which time our first son, Nathan, was born. We completed the new staff training and returned to Ethiopia only to find that our national director, Shimeles Wodajo, was terminally ill. As a result, two weeks after completing new staff training and with no experience of leadership, I was appointed national director for Ethiopia.

As soon as I assumed the national role, and as a task-driven person, I became extremely busy with ministry activities. I often stayed at the office until 11 p.m., making phone calls to church leaders and ministry partners, because cell phones were not yet available and we didn't have a telephone line at home.

In addition, Ethiopian culture places a huge emphasis on social responsibilities, especially for someone with a leadership role in the community. I was expected to attend every wedding and funeral — indeed, every event — often leading in prayer or delivering a speech.

It didn't take long for my discerning wife to realize that we were in trouble. I was too often sacrificing family for ministry or for community responsibilities.

Due to her recommendation, we learned to better divide responsibilities between the two of us to ensure that we maintained balance in ministry, community and family responsibilities. I can honestly say that Shewa's wisdom saved our family.

She is my best partner. Next to God, she is the foundation of our family, ministry and community relationships. She has given her best to raise our children. I believe God has rewarded her efforts by blessing us with children who are humble, God-fearing and talented leaders.

They All Shaped Me

Numerous direct and indirect partnerships have shaped my formative years. My parents didn't have wealth to share with me, but they believed in my future and invested in my development. The community in my village contributed to my upbringing, acting like my own parents and making financial contributions toward my education. Even before my teenage years I learned about the power of partnership by working with the boys in my village.

When I was spiritually bankrupt, God spoke to me on a public bus and sent Teketel Yohannes to restore my relationship with Jesus. Asfaw Keno and the students in my first Bible study group were God's instruments for my spiritual renewal and revival. Even the evil intentions of the communist cadres contributed toward my spiritual development.

At the time when we were going through severe persecution in communist Ethiopia, Christians from around the world came alongside us. In addition to praying for us, they found ways to smuggle in Christian books, tapes, letters and magazines. They provided encouragement and hope. Through their love and generous actions, we learned that we were not alone but members of the worldwide and eternal family of God.

God provided me with a perfect wife who continues to be a great source of wisdom and encouragement in my life and ministry. God used our personal friends, family members and church leaders in our dating, marriage and parenting responsibilities. I am who I am because of the contributions of all these and many other people in my life. Partnerships have shaped not only my story of redemption and formative years but also my early ministry.

Questions for personal and group reflection

1. What were some of the important factors that shaped Bekele's formative years?

2. What factors have shaped your own development?

3. As you think about all these factors, what do you learn about partnerships? And how would that affect the way you view and practice partnerships?

4. Please respond: *One step I will take to implement what I've read in this chapter is* _____

   _____

   _____

   _____

Bekele graduates from high school in 1984, at age 16

*Bekele as a 1987 graduate from Addis Ababa University,
with a degree in statistics and mathematics*

Bekele asks Shewa to marry him.

Shewa signs the document agreeing to marry Bekele.

Bekele and Shewa on their wedding day

CHAPTER 3

My Early Ministry

"Without faith it is impossible to please God" (Hebrews 11:6)

I earned my degree in statistics and mathematics from Addis Ababa University in 1987, at age 19. Then, the country's Federal Ministry of Health recruited me to work at its headquarters as chief information management officer for the National HIV/AIDS Control Program. For nearly six years, my work involved gathering, analyzing and reporting information on the spread and impact of HIV/AIDS in the country. I had opportunities to rub shoulders with national and international scientists, researchers, physicians and policy makers, and I made presentations at educational and scientific conferences.

As I worked with Ethiopians and non-Ethiopians, politicians and civil servants, and with people from diverse cultural and professional backgrounds, I gained insights into the culture of work in government offices as well as cross-cultural leadership. These became important stepping stones in my development.

I enjoyed my job at the Ministry of Health and aspired to become one of the best scientists my country had ever produced, but God had a different plan. He revealed this clearly while I was attending a course at the Centers for Disease Control and Prevention in Atlanta, Georgia, in October 1992. I sensed that God was calling me to serve his purpose in my generation — not my own purposes. Suddenly, the direction of my life completely changed, including my career, ambition and priorities.

That's when I left the Ministry of Health, and my wife and I joined the Great Commission Ministry in Ethiopia. We attended new staff training in Uganda, where God reconfirmed my calling and increased my burden for people who are lost without Christ.

As mentioned earlier, two weeks after returning from this training, I became a national director at age 26. As a statistician, I knew about numbers and probabilities. And as a new staff member of our organization, I had been trained to share the gospel with people and form and lead discipleship groups. But I didn't know how to lead an organization — how to recruit staff, build teams, raise funds, or develop and cast vision. To make things worse, our national director was terminally ill and unable to give me orientation in my new role.

Shimeles, our national director, was a passionate evangelist with national influence — one of the spiritual giants who'd had a significant impact on my life. For several years he had insisted I join the ministry. When he passed away at age 46, I stood next to his grave and watched his body laid to rest, unable to control my tears.

A New Role

My appointment as a national director of our organization in Ethiopia came at one of the most challenging times in the history of our organization in Ethiopia. In addition to our national director being ill for at least a year, senior staff members had left the ministry and the whole organization had less than $50 in the bank. Moreover, some of the older staff members were not happy with my appointment. Understandably, they doubted my ability to lead.

Though not a welcoming place for a new leader, it was a perfect environment to grow in my dependence on God. In that unfriendly environment, my wife and I spent more time in prayer. We poured our hearts out to God, telling him our inadequacies and praying for miracles. We made God our primary partner in his mission.

To orient myself, I focused on the work and legacies of the staff members and the board of directors who had served before me. Within a week, I had studied every document I could find at the national office. The documents included ministry plans of the previous years, ministry and financial reports, and national and international correspondence. Knowing the things that had been done before me, and how they were done, gave me ideas on where and how to start my role.

Through that process I allowed my predecessors to passively mentor me — helping link the past to the present and to the future.

Bold and Crazy

While my wife and I were attending the new staff training in Uganda, I read a book that turned my world right-side up — *Come Help Change the World* by Bill Bright, founder of Campus Crusade for Christ. The book not only gave me vision for the world but also inspired me to believe God for the impossible. As I reflected on the stories of faith presented in the book, my heart was captivated by the possibilities in my home country. God increased my urgency to preach the gospel to those who are lost. I wanted every Ethiopian to experience the love of God — not tomorrow but now.

Clearly, although I was living in Uganda, my heart was already back in Ethiopia. God was preparing me for what lay ahead.

After I studied the history of our organization, Shewa and I met with the few remaining staff members and developed an ambitious national plan. At that time in 1994, about 50 million people lived in Ethiopia, and our plan included:

- dividing the country into 12 regions
- recruiting 300 full-time staff members
- mobilizing churches for the purpose of fulfilling the Great Commission
- raising funds from within and outside the country
- translating the "JESUS" film[17] into 27 major languages spoken across Ethiopia
- acquiring 100 vehicles and two helicopters
- reaching people with the gospel in every village and town

After developing our national plan, the next step was to identify key church leaders in the capital city and invite them to a vision-casting event. Given the existing dire situation of our ministry at the time, I needed courage and confidence from God to share these ideas with church leaders. It was not easy to talk about buying helicopters while struggling to pay monthly bills.

But we believed that God would change our circumstances, and we knew we needed to develop partnerships with individuals, church denominations, local churches and other like-minded mission agencies. Not only did we want their input, but we also knew that this step would generate ownership.

Most church leaders did not know me. When they heard me speak with passion and conviction about reaching every person with the gospel and buying helicopters, some got excited while others doubted. Still, most of those we spoke with endorsed the vision and promised to work with us. We knew that it would take the presence and the power of God to see such ambitious plans fulfilled. This vision-casting was not just an event but a starting point for an exciting journey ahead.

The Tuesday Lunch Strategy

After this citywide event, God gave me another idea: request individual meetings with influential church leaders to talk further. Hence, I developed a strategy called "Tuesday Lunch." Working with my administrative assistant, we lined up individual lunch appointments with leaders throughout 1995 and 1996, primarily with those who had attended the vision-casting event. Every Tuesday for 12 months, I met one leader at a time at some of the best restaurants in the city. Despite our limited ministry funds, I paid for the lunches myself and would not allow my guests to pay. This was my first time to meet most of the leaders in person, and it turned out to be a strategic investment that would soon bear fruit.

In addition to getting to know them personally, I went to those lunches with specific objectives. Before showing up, I did my homework, researching and learning about them and their ministries — including potential resources as well as needs they might have. I was most interested in helping us start working together. As we enjoyed the lunch, I asked three important questions:

- *"Please, could you tell me what God is doing in and through your life and ministry?"* I took the position of a listener and learner, knowing that I can always learn from others. In turn, as each leader shared dreams and hopes, frustrations and discouragements, ministry weaknesses and challenges, I sensed an open door to explore ways we might partner. Then, I would voice my appreciation for the great contribution each was making toward furthering God's kingdom in our nation. In my culture, leaders are often criticized and seldom appreciated.

- *"Can I share what God is doing in my life and ministry?"* They usually replied positively, so I would again share the vision God had laid on my heart. I would quickly identify opportunities, priorities, challenges and threats that I thought were common to both of us. And I used examples of changed lives — people who became effective in ministry after receiving training we offered, donors who made a difference through their giving and churches that were growing rapidly. Frequently, my guest would say, "Bekele, this is exactly what I have been looking for. I want this!"

- *"How can we work together for the glory of God?"* Some leaders immediately had suggestions, but many wanted first to talk about possible costs and opportunities for such a partnership. My first suggestion for pastors was to ask if I could come and preach in their churches. And every pastor said yes.

In these lunch meetings, admittedly, I saw myself as a salesperson, a shrewd manager for the kingdom. I wanted every believer, every pastor and every local church to be involved in the Great Commission. I wanted the gospel of Jesus to be preached in our nation with a sense of urgency, and for churches to be mobilized with great passion. My request did not stop at, "Can I come and preach?" I also asked each pastor if we could train his church members, and I encouraged him to require every trainee to contribute something, even if it was as small as $10.

I invested very little money for the lunches compared to what we harvested as a result. By listening first, I learned about the leaders in the city — about their dreams, passions, opportunities and struggles. Most lunches ended with clear and specific next steps. Sometimes we agreed to meet again. Most of the pastors gave me a specific date to preach in their church. We agreed on when and where to start training. And we identified locations for "JESUS" film showings.

Our city was home to about two dozen mission agencies at the time plus 113 evangelical congregations, which ranged from 25 to 5,000 attendants on Sundays. When I went to preach in those churches, I asked God to give me a message and anoint me with favor. If I did an inferior job in my first opportunity, the churches would not invite me again. I knew my future relationships with the pastors would depend on the quality of my first sermon in their churches.

Thus I prayed, prepared my sermons well and preached with clarity. God gave me wisdom to effectively integrate preaching, vision-casting, appreciation for the work of that local church and a call to action.

In my message, I shared examples of changed lives, showed how trained people were making an impact for the Lord and described how people were giving their resources sacrificially for the Great Commission. My goal was always to bring individuals in my audience to a point of conviction and obedience. I wanted them to say "this is what I want" or "how can I be involved?"

Thanks to the earlier communist persecution, believers were united across denominational barriers. During the persecution, believers from different church backgrounds had gathered in relatively safe places for overnight prayer meetings. If a good sermon was preached in one church, believers in the whole city would hear about it. As a result, we saw ourselves as members of one family — the church of Jesus Christ. And that sense of family still lingered.

I spoke in most of the local churches in the capital city that year, helping believers learn about the Great Commission and commit themselves to it. Whenever I "marketed" the ministry and tried to influence leaders of churches and mission agencies to work together, my motivation was always the Great Commission, the cross of Christ, the bride of Christ and the everlasting kingdom of God. I never wanted to build my own organization nor lift up any name except the name of Jesus and his church.

The evangelical church in Ethiopia grew because of our relationships and our ability to work together. Within four years of the initial vision-casting event, we documented that we had shared the gospel with about 20 million Ethiopians, trained thousands of believers and helped plant hundreds of churches. I also saw God using these relationships far beyond my expectations — he used them to move the body of Christ in Ethiopia to a higher level of spiritual maturity and leadership.

See Appendix A for concrete lessons from my story that can be applied to your leadership journey.

Questions for personal and group reflection

1. What have you learned from Bekele's "Tuesday Lunch" strategy?

2. What attitudes, motives and postures do you think are critical in building healthy partnerships?

3. With whom in your community could you begin to establish relationships, toward a potential future in ministry together?

4. Please respond: *My own version of a "Tuesday Lunch" strategy for building relationships with potential partners in ministry might be:*

_____

_____

_____

_____

*Bekele shortly after college, as a young professional working with
the Ministry of Health, the WHO and the CDC*

Bekele at the CDC in Atlanta, in 1992

Bekele's first team in Ethiopia after he became national director

CHAPTER 4

Partnerships: Untapped Potential

"A foolish man thinks for a day; a wise man thinks for a year"
— Ethiopian proverb

A person who knows how to partner with others is like a miner who discovers a rich vein of gold. But to use the gold, the miner must dig it out of the ground and refine the mineral. It takes a process, patience and hard work. Likewise, developing effective partnerships takes the same effort, and more — you need to add intention, wisdom and humility. Partnerships hold so much untapped potential to unlock hidden resources, especially when we focus on adding value to our partners. Let me share some more lessons I learned while leading the national ministry in Ethiopia.

As I spoke in church after church that first year after our Tuesday Lunch strategy, I was amazed to see how people responded when I presented a clear vision and specific ways to be involved. Most people gave money. Others provided their homes, offices or schools for us to use to organize events free of charge. Still others gave vehicles, clothes or jewelry. Some even gave their wedding rings.[18]

After my sermon, many a local church would give us the regular tithes and offerings collected that Sunday. Other churches allowed us to challenge the congregation for extra donations. To my amazement, every time such a challenge was given, the congregation gave more money than what was collected through tithes and offerings.

We also asked the churches to include our ministry in their annual budgets. Soon, we were receiving regular financial contributions from denominations, local churches and mission agencies. The amount was not as important as the willingness to give.

Why were the churches willing to invest in our ministry? I believe it's because we were willing to work for the growth and multiplication of the churches themselves. Our motive was not to make our organization great but to serve the church of Jesus Christ with humility and sincerity. Through partnerships with both church leaders and other ministry leaders, we not only achieve common goals but also bless one another.

My lunch meeting with the national director of the Bible Society of Ethiopia is a great example.

A Book, a Film and a New Strategy

In 1997, I was eager to explore a partnership with the Bible Society of Ethiopia. Before our appointment, I did a little research and discovered that the organization was printing the Gospel of Luke and distributing it in schools and hospitals and to people in the streets.

I had seen copies of the book torn up, thrown away and trampled. So I thought I could help them be more effective in their distribution. We'd never met before, so as we savored the delicious lunch, we learned about each other and our respective families and ministries. As usual, I asked, "What is God doing in and through you and your organization?" and, "Can I share what God is doing in and through me and *my* organization?"

Then, I said something like, "I am aware of the great work your organization is doing in our country. I know you are printing and distributing the Gospel of Luke. That's really wonderful."

With a sense of affirmation and excitement, I continued, "Do you know that the organizations you and I represent complement one another? You are distributing the Gospel of Luke and we are also distributing the same book."

I observed curiosity in his eyes. So I continued: "You use a print media while we use an electronic media. You have a book, and we have a film. Our organization has created a film on the life of Jesus that is based on the Gospel of Luke, which is available in the major languages of our country. We are showing the film all over the country, and hundreds and thousands of people are trusting in Jesus."

Then I suggested my new strategy for distribution: "We are seeing many people come to Christ through the "JESUS" film, but we don't have Bibles to give to the new believers. What do you think of using your books to disciple new believers? Our teams showing the "JESUS" film could distribute the books all over the country on behalf of the Bible Society of Ethiopia."

My friend got excited about my proposal and asked, "How many copies do you need?"

"Fifty thousand."

He thought they might have 25,000 copies on hand but could provide the remainder, and I asked if I might send over a driver that very afternoon to pick up the first set. (We would receive the remaining 25,000 a few weeks later.)

But before concluding our lunch, I asked him one more question: "As you know, people in our culture usually don't value something they haven't paid for. Would you give me permission to charge a small amount for each book?"

With his permission, we sold the books to people who decided to believe in Jesus after watching the film, knowing that those most serious about their decision would be most willing to pay the small amount.

Through this partnership, both organizations optimized their resources for the glory of God: The Bible Society of Ethiopia provided the books, and the Great Commission Ministry distributed the books to people who were ready to use them. New money was generated to further the kingdom of God in our nation, because the $5,000 generated was invested in a revolving fund that was used to print more ministry materials.

Not "Win-Win" but "Lose-Win"

One goal of our ministry was to foster local ownership in the vision. So we regularly communicated progress and needs to all individuals, churches and mission agencies with whom we partnered.

For example, the Ethiopian new year begins on September 11.[19] So we decided that the first Sunday after the Ethiopian new year would be the "Annual Ministry Day." On that day, for six years (until I left the position of national director), we invited several thousand Christians to gather, including church leaders, local donors, disciples and professionals.

At the event each year, we shared ministry and financial reports of the previous year, including testimonies of changed lives and stories of people who had invested their resources. We also communicated plans and budgets for the following year. And to cultivate a culture of accountability and ownership, we provided copies of financial reports for those who wanted to see them.

In addition to communicating valuable information, these events inspired churches to mobilize their members for ministry; appreciated people who had made outstanding contributions; prayed together for our common challenges (including major spiritual, social, economic and political issues); and provided opportunities for people to invest their time, talent and treasure toward the fulfillment of the Great Commission. As a result, we raised thousands of dollars each year.

More importantly, we worked hard to create an environment in which people felt welcomed, loved and empowered. Our mission agency is part of the church and the church is part of us. So, together, we celebrated God for the great things he was doing in our midst.

In the work of the kingdom, all of us are insiders, owners, contributors and servants. We are together in the glorious work of God; no one is an outsider. God is the owner and the King; we are privileged and favored to work in his kingdom. As we do so, we're not competing with each other, because partnership in the kingdom of God is not win-win but lose-win: We often "lose" so that Jesus wins. And when Jesus wins, all who belong to him will win also.

Unfortunately, sometimes we think and act like the disciples who told Jesus, "Master, we saw someone driving out demons in your name and we tried to stop him because he is not one of us."[20]

Instead, we must know and do what Jesus instructed his disciples in that instance: "Whoever is not against you is for you."

If you lose and I win, there is no benefit to the kingdom of God. But Jesus is glorified when we each can give up our individual drive to "win" over another.

Fifty Lemons

An ancient Ethiopian proverb describes the beauty of partnership: "Fifty lemons are a burden for one person, but fragrance for 50 people." In other words, teamwork can make a difficult task easier. Ministry can be likewise.

For example, we knew that organizing evangelistic dinners for top executives in four- or five-star hotels in Addis Ababa would be expensive and burdensome. So instead of potentially draining our ministry's resources with enormous costs, we invited Christian business leaders to sponsor the guests.

Some business leaders covered the cost of one guest; others covered the cost of an entire table of eight to ten guests. As a result, we presented the gospel to thousands of executives without undue burden.

In addition to covering the costs, these Christian business leaders also re-engaged with their guests after each event and offered to disciple those who had made decisions to follow Christ. And when they recruited more sponsors, they multiplied themselves in another way.

What have I learned through this? When we have a clear vision, pure motive and innovative ideas, the resources we need to fulfill the vision of God are all around us.

See Appendix B for key principles to apply as you create powerful partnerships.

Questions for personal and group reflection

1. What was the Ethiopian proverb Bekele shared, and in what way is it true in your own ministry?

2. Do you believe that your church, city or country has enough resources to fulfill what God is calling you to do? If yes, what would be your responsibility to materialize the resources around you?

3. In what ways did Bekele add value to his ministry partners?

4. Please respond: *One step I will take to add value to those who already partner with me in ministry is* _____

    _____

    _____

    _____

Bekele and Shewa meet Campus Crusade's founders, Bill and Vonette Bright, in 1997.

CHAPTER 5

Local Sustainability

"For where your treasure is, there your heart
will be also" (Matthew 6:21)

From the beginning of my leadership of the Great Commission Ministry, I worked with my team to raise funds from both inside and outside the country. Yet I always knew that our long-term success depended upon the generous giving of Ethiopians. My passion was that our ministry would become self-sustaining — not dependent upon outside sources.

My commitment to this wasn't a matter of pride. I knew the biblical principle that our heart follows our treasure. If we were to invest our "treasures" in seeing Ethiopians come to Christ, then our hearts would become more and more invested as well. And we needed heart investment.

With that in mind, our team knew we needed to see change in some long-held beliefs about giving, while also working hard to raise ministry funds.

Ethiopians Reaching Ethiopians

Hundreds of years ago, when Western missionaries arrived in Ethiopia and in other countries in Africa, they came with financial resources raised from families, friends, local churches and their sending agencies. The missionaries not only had enough resources to sustain their families and work in the mission field, but they also had extra to construct modest churches, schools and hospitals for the people to whom they ministered. We deeply appreciate the foundation laid by those early missionaries.

In most cases the foreign missionaries provided biblical instruction on giving. However, it may be that they failed to teach local churches the importance of supporting and sending their own missionaries. Hence, local believers were not ready to take on that responsibility — a challenge that is common in most African countries even today. Raising financial support for individual missionaries was a new concept to many believers in Ethiopia, though they gave generously for ministry projects.

Shewa and I faced this reality when we were interviewed to join the Great Commission Ministry. During the interview, one of the board members explained to us that Campus Crusade required its staff members to raise financial support. He reminded us that Ethiopia was one of the poorest nations in the world and Ethiopian Christians would not be able to support missionaries. Then he looked at me and asked, "How are you going to survive and serve?"

"I really don't know," I answered, "but I do know that the Lord who called us will provide. Our part is to serve God faithfully and do all we can to raise financial support, but God's part is to provide."

Shewa and I have been with our organization for almost 30 years and have lived in Uganda, Ethiopia, Zimbabwe, South Africa and, now, America. During all those years we lacked nothing. God has raised up partners who have faithfully journeyed with us for a long time.

When I became the national director in Ethiopia, I wanted to recruit many staff members so we could preach the gospel to all Ethiopians. But financial support for our staff members seemed a huge barrier. Hence, with deep conviction, we started an exciting adventure of changing the culture of missionary support among Ethiopian churches — changing one person, one group and one local church at a time.

Our team developed a training program on biblical stewardship. The training included the biblical basis for giving, the role of the Ethiopian church in global mission, the vision of our national ministry and reasons why Ethiopian believers must fund Ethiopian missionaries. We carefully selected people who had the financial means to provide and trained them in resort areas outside the city.

We aggressively implemented the plan, organizing a weekend training almost every month. Before we concluded the training, I explained our national vision and the importance of assuming responsibility to fund God's work in our nation. I attempted to show why it would be wrong for Ethiopian churches to have a vision for sending missionaries abroad but expect the money to come from believers in the West.

I challenged the participants to make financial commitments. Then we diligently followed up those commitments. It was not easy at first; some people thought we were begging for money. But as we continued to train, challenge, follow up and show the results, we observed cultural shifts beginning to take place. The dream of Ethiopian churches sending missionaries abroad by using resources from Ethiopia was becoming a reality!

Many Ethiopian Christians still don't fully understand the responsibility of supporting missionaries financially, but slowly it's beginning to happen, and now an increasing number of missionaries are being supported by Ethiopians. The relationships that I built with church leaders through the Tuesday Lunch became foundational in our efforts to instill the vision of biblical stewardship, raise local resources and recruit national staff.

Ministry Activities as Income

From early on, I was convinced that the Bible teaches us to think and act like businesspeople who lead their businesses with integrity and make profits. I spent time thinking about how to generate local income from ministry activities. It became clear to me that the more resources we generate, the more ministry activities we could implement; and the more ministry activities we implement, the more resources we could generate — a growing cycle of activities and income.

Eventually, we developed more than 20 different ways of raising funds from local sources, and donations in both cash and in-kind gifts flooded into the national office. It was like streams of water flowing from different directions into a lake: Not all streams supplied the same volume of water, but each was important and significant. Regardless of the amount, we received every gift with gratitude to the Lord and to those who provided.

For example, our ministry partnered with a local church to train 20 of its members in evangelism and discipleship for a period of three months. We knew that the training would cost about $1,000. I had already discussed with the pastor the importance of local contributions toward developing locally sustainable ministries and healthy churches. So our plan included several steps:

First, we charged each trainee a registration fee of $10. Second, we taught the trainees how to use the Four Spiritual Laws[21] — an evangelistic booklet we use in our organization — as well as six basic follow-up booklets. We encouraged the trainees to give away the booklets after using them with their contacts, making the message transferable. We gave the trainees a copy of each of the seven booklets but encouraged them to purchase as many copies as they wanted.

In cases where the trainees lacked money, their local church bought the booklets for them. We sold hundreds of copies — about 50 copies per trainee — and generated another $200 in profit.

The training usually took three months to complete. To graduate, each trainee was expected to establish a new discipleship group with at least five new believers. So for our third step, we organized a graduation ceremony with multiple objectives: celebration, vision-casting and fundraising. We asked each trainee to invite his or her disciples and at least 10 other people: friends, family members and potential donors. Meanwhile, we invited leaders of the church as well as leaders from many other churches with whom we wanted to develop similar partnerships.

During the ceremony, I shared the vision and impact of the national ministry, with emphasis on that particular training cycle. A few trainees spoke about the impact of the training and presented their new disciples to the audience, some of whom shared their personal testimonies. Several pastors described the impact of the training, which was our strategy to inspire other pastors in the audience.

Before we concluded the graduation ceremony, I challenged the audience to give. On average, about 200 people attended each event and contributed at least $1,000 per event.

Fourth and finally, each graduate could purchase a special certificate.

All in all, we generated about $1,500 over the course of the training; more than what we needed to cover our costs. If we conducted 20 such trainings in a year, we trained 400 people and raised about $30,000. In this way, training was never a liability for our national ministry but an opportunity to generate more income and equip more people.

Again, our goal was to develop a locally sustainable ministry that would not be dependent on outside resources — a principle that any organization can apply in its own context.

And in reality, the graduation event was not the end of the partnership process but just the beginning. Do you remember the pastors who attended the ceremony from nonparticipating churches? We followed up with them. Some of them called us even before we called them, or they showed up in our office with a desire to work with us. We developed new plans with them while continuing to expand the existing partnerships to new locations.

Ethiopian Coffee Ceremony

Ethiopia has a coffee ceremony tradition observed almost daily by most families. Many Ethiopians drink coffee at least twice a day and multiple cups. Families take turns roasting coffee beans, smelling the aroma, brewing fresh coffee and serving their neighbors. These are social events in which families and friends gather to catch up with one another, enjoy jokes and laughter, and talk about facts and rumors. People with regular jobs socialize on weekends and after hours while others may do so daily. During one of my personal reflection times, I had an idea of how to use the coffee ceremony to generate income for ministry.

I shared with Bisrat Ashebo, our national operations manager, my idea of producing coffee cups, pots, saucers and plates with evangelistic Bible verses printed on them. I had also identified 12 different Bible verses to use, including:

- "For God so loved the world that he gave his one and only Son, that whoever believes in him shall not perish but have eternal life" (John 3:16).

- "I am the way and the truth, and the life. No one comes to the Father except through me" (John 14:6).

- "Salvation is found in no one else, for there is no other name under heaven given to mankind by which we must be saved" (Acts 4:12).

- "If you declare with your mouth, 'Jesus is Lord,' and believe in your heart that God raised him from the dead, you will be saved" (Romans 10:9).

- "Everyone who calls on the name of the Lord will be saved" (Romans 10:13).

Bisrat got excited about the idea and took responsibility to get the job done within three weeks. He went to Hawassa, the only place in the country at that time with a ceramic factory. Three weeks later, hundreds of boxes filled with beautiful cups, pots and saucers arrived at our office. By distributing the items, we sought to accomplish two objectives: offer people an evangelistic strategy and raise funds.

We invited hundreds of believers for training in the evangelistic strategy we had just invented. It was not a complicated strategy; it didn't require one to be bold or to have skills of apologetics: People could purchase the items from our office and then give them as special gifts to their unbelieving relatives, friends and neighbors. Anybody could do that. And who would not like to receive such a beautiful gift from someone who cared deeply for them?

We prayed that as believers used the verses to initiate gospel conversations, the Holy Spirit would reveal the truth about Jesus. At the same time, we creatively generated income to help our ministry invite more people into the kingdom of God.

Talent as Treasure

Let me offer another example. Gospel artists in Ethiopia, especially singers, possess not only unique talents but also popularity and influence. Depending on the singer's fame and the spiritual content of the songs, a single album can generate thousands of dollars.

So our ministry organized a vision-casting event for nationally known gospel singers — solo singers as well as choirs. At the event, I passionately shared the vision of our national ministry. My wife and Million Darsema, the leader of Arts Ministry Ethiopia, were instrumental in mobilizing the artists.

I spoke to the singers about the potential impact they could make for Jesus in our nation and asked them to contribute two or three songs each — songs related to evangelism, discipleship and fulfilling the Great Commission. The singers accepted my proposal and made commitments. Some expressed their appreciation to us for recognizing their talents and giving them opportunities to contribute toward the fulfillment of the greatest purpose of God on earth.

For the next several months, the few studios that existed in the capital city were overwhelmed by the schedule. Many singers received and recorded new songs from the Lord, giving our ministry ownership and distribution rights. From four sets of cassettes, we generated over $20,000 in income and brought inspiration to millions of believers.

God's Available Resources

I disagree with people who believe that they don't have enough resources in their nations. Leaders might fail to recognize their own resources or others' talents, or they may lack the creativity to mobilize both. Talents and resources can remain dormant until the right environment is created and people are invited to be involved in a vision bigger than themselves.

Every task the Lord calls us to do comes with its own provision, and I believe that such provision is not necessarily mobilized from faraway places. However, it takes the ability to see, believe and take the right action. Our churches, organizations and nations are full of people with gifts and talents, so transforming talents into treasure was one of the many strategies of fundraising we implemented in Ethiopia.

Questions for personal and group reflection

1. What are some of the benefits of developing locally sustainable ministries?

2. Which of the creative "ministry activity as income" strategies did you find the most powerful?

3. How does partnership play a role in mobilizing financial and material resources from within your city or nation toward accomplishing God's mission?

4. Please respond: *One step I will take to develop locally sustainable ministry in my context is*_____

_____

_____

_____

*Bekele speaks at the opening of the first branch office of
the Great Commission Ministry of Ethiopia.*

CHAPTER 6

Kingdom Financial Principles

"Remember this: Whoever sows sparingly will
also reap sparingly, and whoever sows generously will also
reap generously" (2 Corinthians 9:6)

O ver a period of four years, our national ministry grew significantly and made an incredible impact in the nation. I believe that this happened because we implemented crucial principles of partnership and generosity, and we wisely managed what God provided. I've already shared about our emphasis on partnership; now let me share four of our most foundational principles of generosity and financial management.

Giving Never Means Less

According to Jesus, "It is more blessed to give than to receive."[22] This does not make sense from a mathematical or economic point of view. When you receive something, you are adding; but when you give away something, you are subtracting from what you have. How could it be more blessed to give than to receive? But when seen from a spiritual and social point of view, it makes perfect sense. Let me tell you why.

First, by giving his only begotten Son, God made it possible for you and me to become his children. By sacrificing his Son on the cross, God has received, and continues to receive, many sons and daughters into his eternal family.

Second, by giving we can make others happier, better, stronger and richer. By giving, we make friends, build allies and multiply our collective effectiveness. When our allies are stronger, we are stronger. When our friends are happier, we are happier. When our partners are growing, we are growing too.

Third, through sacrificial giving we experience joy and fulfillment. I believe that those with spiritual gifts of mercy and giving are some of the happiest Christians; they are involved in doing what God loves to do.

Fourth, giving is like sowing a seed. Every good seed that falls on good soil has great potential for multiplication. Inspired by the Holy Spirit, King Solomon spoke of this principle: "Cast your bread on the surface of the waters, for you will find it after many days."[23] From man's perspective, throwing bread upon the water is foolish and wasteful; but from God's perspective, it's an act of faith and expectation.

Fifth, giving cultivates selflessness, sacrifice and generosity.

Sixth, giving overcomes a poverty mindset.

Seventh, giving is investing in the future — storing treasure in heaven.

As a national ministry in Ethiopia, we joyfully and sacrificially shared with churches and other mission organizations the resources that God gave us. We not only received but we also gave. We believed that every resource we owned came from God and belonged to him, so we managed accordingly — showing love and support to all involved in the Great Commission.

We wrote checks to smaller mission agencies. We let them use our vehicles for their special events free of charge. We were only motivated by the expansion of the kingdom of God in our nation and generation. Our greatest desire was to see every member of the body of Christ becoming healthier, stronger and more fruitful.

I have come to appreciate the fact that giving does not make us poor. On the contrary, the more we give, the more blessed we become. As we continued to give, God kept blessing us. In the five years that I led the national ministry in

Ethiopia, our organization grew from strength to strength. The relational capital we built with church leaders had paid off.

Our partnership was not just monetary but also spiritual — an act of worship to the Lord. As partners, we prayed for each other, we loved each other unconditionally and we praised God for one another's success. Every local church or mission agency I knew had financial needs; none of us had surplus resources. But we were willing to share with and bless one another. We did this because we believed that when we blessed each other, we were blessing the bigger kingdom of God.

Beware a Purse With Holes

Whether you are involved in leading your family, local church or a global organization, you must heed two basic principles of making money: earn more and spend less. Many factors contribute to increased financial expenditures beyond an organization's budget. These could include discontinued funding sources or unexpected emergencies (such as an earthquake or famine), as well as poor planning, lack of accountability, abuse of power or lack of attention to details.

Every penny saved is an asset to an organization. Trying to raise more money while mismanaging what is available is what the Bible describes as putting your money "in a purse with holes in it."[24] It's easy to lose money when you have holes in your purse. Therefore, it is important to identify and close those holes in your organization. God instructed the nation of Israel, "Give careful thought to your ways."[25] Then he exhorted them to handle their business in a way that would please and honor him.

Cutting costs and avoiding wastage of resources is as important as raising new money. For example, we worked hard to assign our personnel in the areas of their giftedness, to optimize the available talents in our organization; and we determined to not create tools and products that already existed within the body of Christ. After all, one organization's *critical needs* are another organization's *available resources*.

Through strategic partnerships, these two elements are brought together and matched toward addressing common challenges. But often, due to lack of knowledge or unwillingness to collaborate, we duplicate activities and waste resources, resulting in less collective strength and impact.

Closing holes in our purse was one of the fundraising strategies we implemented in the Ethiopian national ministry. Whenever we received a check or donation, Tsegaye Sahle (our finance manager) and I laid our hands on the check and prayed over it; we asked God to bless the givers, multiply the gift, and help us manage the resources wisely and efficiently. We thanked God for every donation, regardless of the amount.

We witnessed God multiply the resources. The first year of my leadership as a national director, our ministry income was about $8,000; but four years later, it had reached about $800,000 — a hundred-fold increase. The growth we experienced in the ministry was primarily because of God's favor. But there were also human factors involved, such as faith, creative strategies, effective local partnerships and the strict financial controls we had put in place.

Our ministry grew not only financially but also in ministry activities and results. After a period of four years, we had seen more than 20 million people exposed to the gospel, our staff population had grown from about 12 to 127, the "JESUS" film had been translated into 20 major languages, hundreds of thousands of people had come to Jesus, and thousands of churches had been planted.

Partners are not attracted to an organization with holes in the purse. Partnerships grow in an environment where promises are kept, actions are taken, plans are implemented and resources are used with integrity.

Invest in the Future

Thinking ahead is not listed as one of the spiritual gifts in the Bible. However, it is a gift from God, an important ability for every leader. Although the Bible tells me, "Do not worry about tomorrow,"[26] I often find myself concerned about the future in a positive way; about leaving a legacy, about being better and stronger tomorrow. I want to do something that benefits the coming generations.

What Joseph did during the seven years of prosperity in Egypt inspires me to invest in the future.[27] During the seven years of plenty, Joseph saved 20 percent of Egypt's income for the following seven years of famine. In the same way, we must strategically invest current resources to develop greater capacity for the future.

That's exactly what we did in Ethiopia. At that time, about 80 of our 120 staff members were project workers, employees of the Jesus Film Project*. We paid salaries for those workers through funds donated primarily from North America. When the workers joined our ministry, almost all were high-school graduates, none with a university degree.

We asked ourselves: What would happen to the national ministry if donations from the West ceased to come? How should we raise the educational level of our staff, especially the "JESUS" film team workers? Could we use some of our current resources to build capacity for the future?

In response, we decided to create a "development account," in which we invested 2 percent of all income into our future — into staff development. We provided educational opportunities for all of our "JESUS" film team workers. And because we wanted the staff to have ownership of their own development, we challenged them to contribute about 20 percent of the cost of their personal development.

Most of our staff members took the opportunity and enrolled in part-time college education. Most obtained college degrees a few years later, and some even completed postgraduate degrees, adding value to themselves, to our organization and to the church in Ethiopia. It didn't take long for us to begin reaping the benefits of the investment. The level of confidence and the leadership capability of our staff significantly increased, and the quality as well as the scope of the ministry grew.

As it turned out, after completing their education, some of the staff members left our organization and joined churches and other mission agencies that provided better salaries. But do we regret investing in them? No, not at all. They are still *with us* in God's vineyard. We know that we have added value to the kingdom of God.

We intentionally invested in the future because we knew that our ministry's future health, performance and productivity depend on what we are doing today.

Putting aside 2 percent of our income wasn't an easy decision, because paying for staff education seemed to compete with the urgency of proclaiming the gospel. But in order to ensure the quality and sustainability of the proclamation of the gospel, it was necessary to invest in the development of organizational capacity.

Furthermore, our concerns about the longevity of external funding became a reality a few years later. The Jesus Film Project in America decided to stop funding the film teams, creating panic in many national ministries, especially in the developing world. Many countries had to lay off some of their best field personnel. But it was a different story in Ethiopia. By the time the Jesus Film Project changed its priorities and quit funding film teams, 54 of our "JESUS" film workers were ready to become missionary staff and raise their own financial support locally. As a result, they were able to continue their ministry responsibilities.

As I write this, most of these workers in Ethiopia are leading national church-planting initiatives. They have the confidence and capability to work with church leaders, to develop partnerships, to cast vision, to train and coach church planters, to mobilize resources, and to initiate and lead national projects.

Poverty Is No Match for God's Spiritual Wealth

Most of the world remembers Ethiopia's famine years.[28] Indeed, during these early years of ministry, the World Bank reported the country as one of the poorest in the world.[29] But by thinking creatively and acting boldly, empowered by the Holy Spirit, we mobilized sufficient financial and material resources from within our country *during those same years.*

I am convinced that God would do the same in other countries whose material poverty is no match for God's spiritual wealth.

I would soon undertake one of the greatest adventures in my leadership journey — a higher-level partnership than I had ever dreamed possible. Through what we would call Operation Philip, I learned that clear vision and bold leadership attracts people. And when people are attracted, resources become available. When people and resources are mobilized, the mission is accomplished. When the mission is accomplished, people are fulfilled and God is glorified.

Questions for personal and group reflection

1. What did you learn from the author's four kingdom financial principles?

2. What additional principle(s) would you add to that list?

3. The author stated that "material poverty is no match for God's spiritual wealth." Do you agree? Why or why not?

4. Please respond: *One step I will take to implement what I've read in this chapter is* _____

_____

_____

_____

CHAPTER 7

Operation Philip

"What is impossible with man is possible
with God" (Luke 18:27)

Back in 1998, Christians unleashed the power of partnership in the Ethiopian capital of Addis Ababa — then a city of about 3 million people, including hundreds of thousands of day laborers who had flooded in to search for jobs. The body of Christ came together for Operation Philip, a multi-strategy evangelistic campaign designed to reach the city with the gospel. At just 30 years of age, I had the privilege of initiating and coordinating this 52-day campaign characterized by bold faith and creativity.

I have led many national and multinational projects, but Operation Philip remains the highlight of my life so far. God used it to stretch my faith, enlarge my vision and develop my leadership skills, especially in the areas of mobilization and strategic partnerships.

At the time, Addis Ababa was divided into 26 districts with 252 smaller administrative units known as *kebeles*, or localities, created by the communist government to closely monitor day-to-day life and activities. The yoke of communism had been broken seven years earlier, but the administrative units remained the same.

Operation Philip was birthed when another member of the Great Commission Ministry of Ethiopia approached me with a question: "Bekele, about five years ago we implemented a project to reach one of the 26 districts in the city. What would you think of reaching the whole city with the gospel?"

I thought about that question over the next few days, and as I did, I felt a growing burden for the city. Then I started praying with my wife, Shewa, asking God for confirmation and guidance. Our staff team was still small — we had 38 workers, including staff members who worked as security guards, drivers and office management personnel, with most of us under 30 years of age.

Yet I soon sensed God confirming the vision in my heart, and I began writing out the essential processes and strategies. Then in December 1997, I took our national leadership team on a three-day planning retreat to Hawassa, a beautiful city in Southern Ethiopia.

We spent the first day worshipping the Lord, singing, praying and listening to the Word of God. In preparation for our planning time, I had asked Abebe Abate, one of our newest staff members, to share from the Word of God. I had no idea that God would use him to confirm the vision, because I had not yet shared the plan with any of our staff.

Abebe passionately spoke on Isaiah 41:8-16, emphasizing that we should not be afraid of anything. He affirmed that God is always with us and challenged us to believe God for the impossible and prepare for great exploits. I was encouraged by the message and convinced it was time to believe God for great things.

Inspired by Abebe's message and leaning on God's wisdom, we developed an impossible plan that only God could accomplish: a plan to reach the whole city of Addis Ababa with the gospel in 52 days. We gave ourselves a period of six months to prepare.

Abebe would soon tell me: "Bekele, I am here to support you in every way I can. The northwest region of Ethiopia that you gave me to lead is not enough for me. I am ready to take more regions."

He was a dear friend and a great source of encouragement. But he was not fortunate enough to see the fulfillment of the vision. Five weeks after our planning meeting, Abebe died in a terrible car accident while on a ministry trip in northern Ethiopia.

It was the first visible spiritual attack on us as well as on the vision. Our hearts were broken. We had his body airlifted to Addis Ababa, where it was laid to rest. He left behind his wife, Berhan, plus three sons and a daughter ranging from 5 months to 5 years.[30]

The Preparation

Inspired by the story of the evangelist Philip in Acts 8:26-40, we named the campaign "Operation Philip: Restoring the Old Mission." In the story, an Ethiopian eunuch was fulfilling his religious duties of visiting the Holy Land and reading the Scriptures but did not understand what he was reading. It took the Holy Spirit and the evangelist Philip to address the man's spiritual problem. Similarly, of the 3 million people living in Addis Ababa at the time, more than 85 percent claimed to be Christians. But if they were confronted with the content of the gospel message, I believe many of those "Christians" would ask the same question as the Ethiopian eunuch: "How can I [understand], unless someone explains it to me?" [31]

Our team then studied the religious and sociodemographic composition of the city. Addis Ababa hosts 82 of Ethiopia's 92 ethnic groups, so reaching the city with the gospel would be like reaching almost the whole country. The membership of the city's 113 evangelical churches totaled about 3 percent of the city's population, while the Ethiopian Orthodox Church claimed about 82 percent, the Muslims 8 percent, the Catholics less than a percent and others about 6 percent.

We chose 52 days as our goal for reaching the city, motivated by how Nehemiah and the Israelites completed the rebuilding of the broken walls of Jerusalem in that time frame. We established prayer teams in every local church and *kebele*, and even in schools, boardrooms and coffee shops.

Then we mapped out the whole city by demographic, geographic and socioeconomic strata, creating strategies of evangelism, discipleship and training for each segment of society. The main strategies included:

- personal, group, home-to-home and mass evangelism

- indoor and outdoor "JESUS" film showings as well as video and literature distribution

- distribution of food and clothing

- preaching of the gospel message at Sunday worship services

- executive outreach dinners, and business and leadership seminars

- training and mobilization conferences for women, college students, children and youth

- music festivals, drama and painting

We identified and trained leaders for each segment of society and each strategy. We envisioned equipping every Christian to share the gospel effectively; exhorting every individual believer, local church, mission agency and denomination to give resources sacrificially; and encouraging all the churches to focus on the kingdom of God and work together. We developed a macro plan for the city, but each task force and sub-task force developed its own detailed plan.

The next step after creating the overall plan was to cast the vision. We organized various vision-casting events. The first was for our own staff members, which was critical to ensure that they clearly understood the vision and had the conviction, commitment and capacity to lead it.

Before we went out to raise money from churches and individuals, we had to sow the first seeds ourselves. In terms of material resources, our staff didn't own much. However, like the widow whom Jesus commended for giving her two copper coins,[32] our staff gave sacrificially.

The next step was to train our staff to clearly communicate the vision. We prepared materials for them to use and rehearsed answering potential questions people might ask.

Opposition

In spite of the hardships experienced during the communist regime, Ethiopian evangelical churches had thrived during the 17 years of persecution. It was estimated that the Ethiopian evangelical church grew from less than a million to about 8 million members during those difficult years. God also used that hostile political environment to refine and strengthen the church.

As noted earlier,[33] during those years we refused to let denominational barriers divide us, but worshipped together and loved one another. Basically, we knew only one church, the church of Jesus Christ. All the believers were like one large family willing to die for one another and for the sake of Christ. However, after the collapse of the communist government, the churches did not know how to handle the new religious freedom, and they began to erect barriers among themselves.

Churches that had survived the communist persecution felt more righteous than churches established afterward. Instead of embracing and mentoring, the leaders of older churches became cautious about the personalities and ministries of the leaders of younger churches. Such an approach eventually resulted in two major groupings of churches: older churches that were part of the Ethiopian Evangelical Churches Fellowship and post-communism churches waiting to be embraced as members of the fellowship.

But the vision we wanted to see fulfilled in the city would require the involvement of every church and every believer. We started by organizing separate vision-casting events, one for the older churches and another for the younger churches. When some leaders of the older churches learned about our intention to involve younger churches in the project, they threatened to stop working with us. But we insisted that we must all embrace one another with unconditional love, maintain kingdom perspective and focus on fulfilling the mission of God together. After several meetings, prayers and negotiations, most leaders showed willingness to work together. But some church leaders were still reluctant and gave us reasons like:

- You and your staff are too young and inexperienced, so you don't have the capacity to pull off such a big project.

- Such a huge campaign will attract another wave of persecution against the church.

- It is impossible to bring the churches together.

- Our country is poor, and you will not be able to raise the $500,000 needed.

- Reaching the whole city in 52 days is an impossible task.

- The Evangelical Churches Fellowship has not yet approved the leaders of the task forces you have appointed.

Because of such concerns, three of the five senior leaders I had selected to be my advisers declined. One invited me to his office and gave me seven reasons why I should forget about the vision. I was disappointed. But at the same time, that particular meeting increased my dependence on God, as well as my determination to lead the project.

In this case, we overcame the concerns by praying together, talking about the challenges, using the Word of God as our spiritual authority and building on our existing relationships with church leaders. As a result, the churches stood ready to implement the impossible task.

But then, just a few weeks before our July 8, 1998, launch date, some notable national newspapers began writing against us. We were labeled as a threat to national security. At the same time as we were casting the vision of Operation Philip, Ethiopia was preparing for a war against Eritrea — one of the senseless wars that took place from May 1998 to June 2000 and claimed the lives of up to 120,000 people on both sides. One newspaper described Operation Philip as an ideological war waged by Eritrea against Ethiopia and insisted that the Ethiopian government take strong action against our work.

The reason for linking Operation Philip with the Ethiopian-Eritrean war was bizarre: The name of the patriarch of the Eritrean Orthodox Church during 1998–2000 was Philip or Philipos. Hence the newspaper wrote, "Operation Philip is an ideological war led by patriarch Philip of Eritrea to stop Ethiopians from going to war."

Fortunately, once Ethiopian national security verified the facts, we continued with the preparations.

In partnership with the Ethiopian Evangelical Christian Workers Fellowship, we established a house of prayer. There, believers gathered to pray for the city 24 hours a day, seven days a week. Although the house of prayer belonged to the Christian Workers Fellowship, our ministry covered the cost of rental for two years. Every day at the house of prayer, people gathered to pray in shifts of six hours each.

In addition, more than 3,700 people prayed in 252 other locations across the city, interceding for the salvation of souls. Several believers also regularly prayed for *me,* that I would not lose focus and would have strength to lead — just as Aaron and Hur held up the hands of Moses for Joshua to win the battle.[34]

Taxis, Buses and Bars

On July 8 as the project officially launched, you could sense excitement in the city. "Operation Philip starts today!" read the front-page headline in one news-paper as it tried to stir up opposition to the work. Individuals, families, groups and churches prayed for believers to preach the gospel with boldness, for God to display his power and save people from their sins, for churches to be united, and for the protection of workers.

During those 52 days, we trained about 10,000 believers in evangelism and discipleship in 22 locations across Addis Ababa, and I wrote a motivational letter to every person involved. We then sent the trainees out in groups of two to pray and to witness for Jesus in different sections of the city — taking our cue from Chapter 3 of the Book of Nehemiah.

Families invited friends and neighbors to their homes, showing the "JESUS" film, sharing testimonies and leading discipleship groups. In task forces, cell groups and local churches we all studied Nehemiah, uniting our hearts and learning about ministry strategies.

Throughout the campaign, in places as varied as taxis, music stores, buses and bars, it was common for people to hear, "Have you heard of the Four Spiritual Laws?" as a way to open up conversations about the gospel. Here are just a few of the creative ways we touched Addis Ababa with that gospel:

- Christians showed the evangelistic "JESUS" film over 800 times in churches and schools, in offices and executive boardrooms, in restaurants, and in the open air. We created a six-minute audiocassette gospel presentation with an invitation to receive Christ, and then we trained Christian taxi drivers to play the cassettes in their taxis. The tape started with that familiar question: "Have you heard of the Four Spiritual Laws?"

- Thousands of people attended evangelistic music festivals and dramas organized by professional artists.

- The staff of World Vision Ethiopia fasted and prayed during their lunch hour every Friday — contributing several thousand dollars to the campaign that they would have otherwise spent on lunch. The staff also used that time to share the gospel in the streets.

- Some believers loaned their cars for the entire duration of the project while they used public transport for themselves.

- Local churches mobilized food and clothing distributions for the needy. Wherever food was served, spiritual food was also presented.

- More than 400 professional and amateur artists participated in a competition to paint a story from one of the Gospels. When we announced the winners, most of the artists attended the ceremony, giving us one more opportunity to present the gospel. We later generated income by selling some of the paintings.

- We planned outreach dinners and leadership seminars for top executives, business leaders, professionals and government officials.

God in Pursuit

Throughout our campaign, we often received emergency phone calls about brothers and sisters who were seriously injured, arrested or imprisoned because of sharing the gospel. But on one particular night, we had a different type of emergency: Our keynote speaker for an executive event canceled.

We had invited every ambassador and top government executive in the country, including the prime minister. And more than 200 had RSVP'd that they would attend. Scheduled to speak was Brigadier General Godfrey Miyanda, former vice president of the Republic of Zambia and then minister of education. He was a born-again believer.

One night before the event, however, the Zambian embassy in Addis Ababa informed me that General Miyanda would not be coming. They didn't tell me the reason. It was around 10 p.m. and I was still in my office with a few leaders, making final preparations. So we knelt and asked God to intervene.

While we were praying, God gave me some ideas. One was to call Zambia and find out why the trip was canceled. I learned that the matter was in the hands of the country's president, Frederick Chiluba. He was not comfortable with the minister traveling abroad, most likely because General Miyanda was establishing a new political party.

We began to pray yet again. And then I called Zambia to ask for the direct fax line to the president. A few years earlier, when Mr. Chiluba had become president, he had declared Zambia a Christian nation — which I mentioned in my fax message to the president. I closed by "kindly asking Your Excellency to intervene in this situation and encourage General Miyanda to come."

After confirming that the fax had gone through, we left the office around midnight. Just as King Xerxes could not sleep on the night God wanted to intervene in the affairs of the Jews in Babylon,[35] the Zambian president, I believe, experienced something similar that night. So he was awake to read our fax message.

The next morning, the Zambian ambassador called: "General Miyanda is arriving this morning. Our president has released him. Please come to the VIP room at the airport to welcome him."

That evening, General Miyanda spoke on "Nation Building: Quest for Excellence in Leadership" to 280 top leaders gathered at the Sheraton Addis. After his message, Dela Adadevoh, a scholar from Ghana and my supervisor at the time, presented the gospel and invited people to respond. About 10 percent of those present indicated that they had prayed to receive Christ. At another similar Operation Philip event attended by 420 top professionals, 144 prayed to receive Christ.

Over the 52 days, the task force leaders continued to meet every week for evaluation and correction. We heard stories of faith, boldness, salvation and healing, but also stories of brothers and sisters who were beaten and imprisoned. We praised God for the miracles and prayed for the challenges. We assessed the ministry situations, allocated resources, identified and solved the problems we could, and prayed for those we could not.

During Operation Philip, it was common for us to meet individuals who said, "Jesus is everywhere in this city. This is my fifth time to hear about Jesus today. What is going on in this city? Maybe God is pursuing me until I say yes to Jesus."

Indeed, the windows of heaven were wide open, the Spirit of God was hovering overhead, just as he had in the first pages of the Bible,[36] and people were running to Jesus. Little children were leading gangsters to the Lord, the hopeless were finding hope, and the prayers of thousands of people were bringing answers from heaven.

See Appendix C for a step-by-step guide to help design your organization's own partnership process.

Questions for personal and group reflection

1. Which critical steps highlighted in this chapter might you use toward developing and communicating your own vision?

2. Why is it so important to ensure that the vision has strong ownership within your organization before casting it to other stakeholders, and how do you ensure that ownership?

3. What do you learn from Bekele's approach to discovering and unleashing creativity and potential resources for extraordinary results?

4. Please respond: *The first three steps I would like to take toward developing the vision God has been putting in my heart are:* _____

_____

_____

_____

Bekele casts vision for Operation Philip.

CHAPTER 8

Operation Philip: Results

*With the help of our God we dared to tell you
his gospel in the face of strong opposition"
(1 Thessalonians 2:2)*

Then the 52 days were over, and we gathered reports from various task forces. What God had done through Operation Philip was just amazing. When the reports were compiled, more than 1.6 million people had heard the gospel, with about 49,000 people reporting that they had prayed to receive Christ. The opposition was strong, and the battle was fierce. But God gave us faith, favor and victory. Jesus' words to Peter rang true: "I will build my church; and the gates of Hades will not overpower it."[37]

It is impossible to describe all the deeds of God during Operation Philip, but here are a few stories. . . .

Amazing Stories

Zerihun Mekuria

I have a passion to preach the gospel to street boys, for I myself was once a street boy saved by the grace of God. So, one night during Operation Philip, my friend and I went out after midnight to share the gospel. At around 2 a.m., we found 15 street boys and shared the gospel with them. We asked them to raise their hands if they were ready to receive Jesus, and all hands went up.

As we were about to lead them in prayer, suddenly we got surrounded by policemen who pointed guns and commanded us not to move. After a quick silent prayer in my heart, I told the policemen we were peaceful men only sharing the love of God. We saw God's immediate intervention: The policemen left us, and all 15 street boys accepted Jesus.

Zebasil Tekeba

My friend Haileyesus Debele and I were praying for an opportunity to preach the gospel to law enforcement officers in one of the prisons. But it was impossible to get an open door. One day, we showed the "JESUS" film at my friend's house. After that, I went home and did not know that the police had come and arrested my friend for showing the film. Amazingly, he was taken to the same prison in which we had been asking God to open the door for us to preach. Now I thought, "Maybe this is the opportunity we have been waiting for." So, with two copies of the "JESUS" film DVD and several copies of the Four Spiritual Laws booklet, I went to visit my friend in the prison.

Then I told the police, "I have the film my friend showed yesterday. My friend didn't do anything wrong. Maybe you have never watched the film for yourselves, and you would like to watch it now."

I offered to show the film and they agreed to watch. Interestingly, they called my friend from the prison and asked him to sit with them and watch the film. All the police officers watched the film and decided to release my friend. We were amazed by how God has answered our prayers to preach the gospel to the law enforcement officers.

Eden Woldegabriel

I was part of the youth mobilization task force. One day, after completing our witnessing assignment, we gathered to thank the Lord for what he had done. Then, for some reason we decided to continue with witnessing and went to share the gospel with a witch doctor. With no objection, the witch doctor and all his assistants heard the gospel. But none of them accepted Jesus.

As we left the witch doctor's house, we were talking about what we did. Then suddenly many people surrounded us. We preached the gospel to them also and 15 of them accepted Jesus.

Bethlehem Demissie

As part of the youth mobilization task force, I was assigned to witness in the Akaki area along with two brothers. While I was sharing Christ with one person, my teammates walked away to witness to another person. Suddenly about 100 people surrounded me. From the crowd, a huge man walked toward me shouting, "Stop. If you don't, you will lose all your teeth." Realizing how tense the situation was, I tried to leave the scene. But about 10 people started pulling and pushing me.

With all my energy, I shouted back, "In the name of Jesus!" Then the presence of God came over us, the crowd dispersed, and I started walking toward a nearby church. Surprisingly, for no reason, the main instigator as well as several others followed me to the church and gave their lives to Jesus. They also asked me for forgiveness.

Addisu Nigatu

I was part of the task force responsible for reaching prostitutes, especially those who went out at night and waited for customers on street corners. We were sent out two by two and given a specific section of the city. One night, my friend and I approached two women; one was sitting and weeping while the friend tried to comfort.

When we started sharing the gospel, they called over another friend, who was standing at another location. All three women prayed to receive Christ. Then they told us the story of the woman who was weeping: She had lost hope in her life and was contemplating suicide that night. She carried a rope with her. By the time we arrived, the friend was begging her not to commit suicide. But the love of God changed her life forever.

Tigist Elias

Before the campaign started and even before the training, I had three days of fasting and prayer, asking God to prepare me to be his instrument. During my prayer, I asked God to use me to bring 52 people to Jesus, one salvation a day over the period of the campaign. But on the 38th day of the campaign, I reached my goal of seeing 52 people come to Jesus through my witnessing.

Also, two weeks into the campaign and as I was witnessing in the street, two police officers arrested me and put me in jail. I was in jail for five hours but continued witnessing there. The police officers thought they would stop the work of God. But no one can stop the work of God. Elders from my church came to the prison to appeal for my release, but actually I wanted to stay there and tell more people about Jesus. I was filled with the joy of the Lord. When the police realized I was telling the prisoners about Jesus, they let me go home.

A City Shaken by the Spirit

On September 6, 1998, we celebrated what God had done through Operation Philip. Task force leaders carefully considered people who had made significant contributions and invited about 3,000 of them. But because of the impact of the campaign, more than 10,000 people showed up and we needed to set up multiple TV screens outside the church auditorium.

We heard reports about the unity of the church, the power of prayer and of sacrificial giving, and the courage of believers to share the gospel in an antagonistic environment. And we listened to testimonies of changed lives. We gave certificates of appreciation to those who had excelled in their work and to churches that had mobilized their entire congregations and allowed us to raise funds during their Sunday services.

The whole city was shaken by the power of the Holy Spirit and the audacious actions of believers. We documented 1.65 million people who had heard the gospel during the 52 days, with 49,000 decisions for Christ. But there may have been many more, since Operation Philip had become a massive movement beyond our control. We lost track of what was happening and who was doing what.

A significant number of believers from the younger churches participated — those churches not part of the national evangelical fellowship. While I was giving my report, the Holy Spirit prompted me to do something unexpected: I asked all who came from churches not included in the national fellowship to stand. Probably 10 to 20 percent of the audience stood.

I asked them to remain standing and invited those who were sitting to look at them. Filled with the Holy Spirit, I declared, "As of today, the walls of division have been broken down. Those who are standing are brothers and sisters whose sins have been washed away by the blood of the Lamb. They are going to inherit the same kingdom that we are going to inherit. We all have one church, one Father, one kingdom and one fellowship.

"Now, those of you who are sitting, please could you stand up and hug those who are standing around you and tell them that we are one and we love one another?"

For the next several minutes, people were hugging, cheering, weeping and praising the Lord. Some people, overwhelmed by the presence of God, knelt to worship. The walls of division came tumbling down. The attitude of seniority began melting away. We declared our oneness in Jesus Christ. There must have been great joy in heaven as well.

While all this was taking place, most of the senior church leaders sat in front of me, occupying the first three rows of the auditorium. I was under the control of the Holy Spirit and didn't care if I would be excommunicated from the church. After the celebration, I heard that while many leaders supported me, some were upset and asked each other, "Who is he to make such a statement?"

It was not me who did all that, but Jesus Christ — he who had prayed for our unity in the Gospel of John.[38] I don't know why we focus on our differences. I don't know why we can't view our differences as unique gifts from the Lord and focus on the mission of God. I don't know why we can't humble ourselves and love one another unconditionally.

In heaven, we will all have one name, the Bride of Jesus; we will all have one leader, King Jesus; and we will all have one denomination, the eternal kingdom of God. So, why can't we begin practicing that now?

Time to Move

A week after the celebration, the national directors of Campus Crusade for Christ in the region gathered at the Hilton Hotel in Addis Ababa. The main agenda was to choose a successor to Dela Adadevoh, my supervisor and leader for the ministry for Southern and Eastern Africa. He had been appointed as a global vice president for our organization and was in the process of relocating to our global office in Orlando, Florida.

In that meeting, I was chosen to succeed Dela, and I soon began preparing for our relocation to Harare, Zimbabwe. I had led the national ministry of Ethiopia for only five years, five short but fulfilling years. During those years, our staff population grew from about 10 to 127; we reached more than 20 million people with the gospel; our financial resources significantly increased; my relationship with church leaders was at its peak; the Great Commission Ministry became one of the most fruitful and influential ministries in the country; we translated the "JESUS" film into 20 major languages and were showing it throughout the country; and hundreds of thousands of people came to Christ.[39]

Lessons on Leadership

Operation Philip provided me an amazing opportunity to grow as a leader. Through our unity as Ethiopian believers, we were able to do more than any one organization could have done. Most of the financial resources were raised from within the country. God used the campaign to impart vision to thousands of young people. In addition, I have met many pastors and evangelists who confirmed God's calling in their life during Operation Philip and ordinary Ethiopians all over the world who came to Jesus during those 52 days.

Wherever I go in the world and speak at Ethiopian congregations, I ask people to raise their hands if they were part of Operation Philip. Even in the farthest places, like Melbourne, Australia, at least 10 percent of the congregation raise their hands.

Three months after I stood in front of church leaders on the day of celebration and declared, "As of today, the walls of division have been broken down," the Evangelical Churches Fellowship of Ethiopia officially accepted the younger churches into the Fellowship. We may see the full impact of Operation Philip only in eternity.

Before moving to Zimbabwe and assuming my new role, I handed over the responsibility of the Ethiopia ministry to Getachew Beyoro, one of the key leaders of Operation Philip. Without knowing what the Lord had in store for us, Shewa and I, along with our three children, relocated to Zimbabwe in August 1999. There, we found different food, weather, people and culture. We left behind our families, friends and church in Ethiopia, but we took with us God and his promises, the experiences of leading the ministry in Ethiopia, and the lessons we learned through Operation Philip.

Questions for personal and group reflection

1. What do you learn from the design and implementation of Operation Philip?

2. Why do you think people are attracted to a vision bigger than themselves?

3. Is God calling you to attempt something big that cannot be accomplished with the resources you have? If so, what is it?

4. Please respond: *The trusted friends I will ask to come alongside me, as I strive to be obedient to this call, are* _____

_____

_____

_____

A celebration of what God did during Operation Philip

CHAPTER 9

Operation Sunrise Africa

"If you have faith like a grain of mustard seed,
you will say to this mountain, 'Move from here to there,'
and it will move, and nothing will be impossible for you"
(Matthew 17:20)

Africa is an incredibly diverse continent, with as many as 3,000 ethnic groups and 2,000 languages. The continent's landmass is larger than the combined landmasses of the United States, China, India and much of Europe,[40] and it would take at least 10 hours to fly from Cairo to Cape Town or Somalia to Senegal.

After a four-hour nonstop flight from Addis Ababa, Shewa and I, along with our three children (all under age 5) and a niece, landed at Harare airport in Zimbabwe. Two families greeted us at the airport and took us to our new home in Mount Pleasant, a beautiful suburb in northern Harare where we would live for the next six years. We so appreciated this warm welcome from David and Christine Dawanyi, and Ken and Patty Borgert. David served as Zimbabwe's national director for Campus Crusade at the time, and Ken as director of operations at our regional office.

The Borgerts, American missionaries who had moved there from Swaziland three years earlier, became our cultural guides and made our settling-in process easier and more enjoyable. Together, we explored the beauty of Zimbabwe, including Victoria Falls, Nyanga National Park, Vumba Gardens and Lake Kariba — the world's largest manmade lake and reservoir.[41]

Zimbabwe would become one of our favorite places in the world, with its stunning scenery, luxury lodging, breathtaking national parks and diverse wildlife, which includes majestic elephants and the fourth-largest black rhino population in the world.

Harare, Zimbabwe's capital, used to be one of the most beautiful cities in Africa. Then around 2005, Zimbabwe's economy collapsed. The government's poorly thought-through land-redistribution policy resulted in international economic sanctions, internal unrest and reduced national productivity. Zimbabweans who should have benefited from the land-reform policy were unable to make the best use of the land because they lacked the necessary training, tools and financial resources.

We found Zimbabwe a fascinating place. When we landed in the country, Zimbabweans were still celebrating their independence from the British Empire, achieved nine years earlier. For the first time in our lives, we saw signs such as "Private Property" — one of the legacies of that Western colonization.[42] Overall, we found Zimbabweans to be a peaceful people who avoided conflict unless forced to react.

We also discovered that Zimbabwe was ahead of Ethiopia in many ways, including education, health care, industrialized agriculture, roads and other economic infrastructure. President Robert Mugabe led Zimbabwe to significant socioeconomic progress during the first 10-15 years of his 37-year regime (1980-2017).[43]

When we arrived, the country boasted one of the best educational and health-care systems in Africa. As a person with seven degrees in arts, administration, education, science and law, Mugabe understood the role education plays in national development. As a result, he established primary schools in every community, which provided quality education along the lines of the British system. The national literacy rate stood at 97 percent. And medical care was excellent and inexpensive — our family of six paid a monthly premium of just $100 for medical benefits.

A New Environment

After unpacking suitcases and learning the location of such important places as the post office, the electric company, the immigration department and telecommunications companies, I reported to my new office and met my new team. The team had been together for at least three years — a mixture of Zimbabweans, Kenyans, Ugandans, Malawians and Americans. I was the only newcomer as well as the youngest member, and I had no experience with cross-cultural leadership.

As a regional leadership team, we were responsible to coordinate the work of Campus Crusade in Southern and Eastern Africa including the Indian Ocean Islands — 23 countries total, with about the same population as the United States.

The English language was not widely spoken in my home country of Ethiopia, and as a result, my ability to communicate in English was limited. I had also heard that some of my new team members were not happy with my appointment. These factors signaled the potential challenges ahead, which didn't take long to appear. I received direct criticism and harsh words from some of my team members. They compared my leadership style with that of my predecessor, they took issue with my speed of action and they disliked my tendency to focus on results.

Nevertheless, through these challenges I learned an important lesson: Even in the face of hostility and rejection, you can grow as a leader if you focus on the positives. God used the initial challenging environment of that team to shape my character and prepare me for greater things to come.[44] During those years Shewa and I prayed more, grew in our dependence on God, read more books on leadership — especially how to work with different personalities — and learned the importance of enduring hardship.

Fifty Times More

One day in the year 2000, after the dust of adjusting to my new environment and team had settled, I was praying and asking God for his plans for the region. I heard a divine whisper in my heart: "Fifty times more." I didn't understand at the time what it meant, but a supernatural joy filled my heart. As I continued to pray, it became clear that God was calling me to design and lead a project that was 50 times bigger than the one I had facilitated about a year earlier in Addis Ababa.

Since Operation Philip had aimed to reach one city in Ethiopia, then "fifty times more" must mean 50 cities, I thought. God wanted to stretch my faith and take the gospel to people who lived in the largest 50 cities in the countries of Southern and Eastern Africa. Through prayer and the guidance of the Holy Spirit, I started writing the vision.

My conviction grew almost daily. Oswald Chambers in his book *My Utmost for His Highest* writes, "The one who says 'Yes, Lord, but . . .' is the one who is fiercely ready, but never goes. . . . When once the call of God comes, begin to go and never stop going."[45]

Accordingly, I had a strong conviction that we needed to move forward and never hesitate over whether the idea was from the Lord.

By the time I had finished writing all that was in my heart, I was overwhelmed by the magnitude of the task. It became a vision to reach 50 million people with the gospel in 50 major cities in 50 days in 23 countries. The cities stretched from Cape Town, South Africa, to Asmara, Eritrea, and from Windhoek, Namibia, to Port Louis, Mauritius.

The rallying cry of the vision, which became known as "Operation Sunrise Africa" or simply "Operation Sunrise," was simple: Help accelerate evangelism, discipleship and missions in Southern and Eastern Africa through a 50-50-50 strategy. The vision of Operation Sunrise Africa was inspired by a Bible verse: "But for you who revere my name, the sun of righteousness will rise with healing in its rays. And you will go out and frolic like well-fed calves."[46]

We desired the same healing, freedom, righteousness and joy for every person in those 50 cities. God has promised those benefits to everyone who reveres his name.

Seeking Solutions

To develop the vision further, our team went on a three-day prayer and planning retreat to a beautiful resort area in Zimbabwe. As I prepared to facilitate the planning time, I created seven discussion questions to guide the process.

The first question concerned identifying major opportunities and challenges within our organization, our nations, the church in Africa and the continent as a whole. We looked at the socioeconomic, cultural and political environment of Africa vis-à-vis the depth and impact of Christianity in the continent. Through the process, we realized that some of the greatest challenges in Africa included poor leadership, poverty, the spread of HIV/AIDS, civil wars, corruption, mismanagement of resources and a lack of quality education.

Bill O'Donovan, an American missionary who had served in Africa for more than 30 years, had similarly summarized the continent's challenges in a book published a few years earlier, asking poignantly: "What kind of future does Africa have? What, if anything can the people of God do?"[47]

Moreover, in 1973 Africa had about 100 million people who claimed to be Christians. By the year 2000, when we were developing the Operation Sunrise vision, that number had grown to almost 400 million, about 50 percent of Africa's population. But in the face of such social ills as ethnic conflict, genocide, government corruption and mismanagement of resources, many questioned the impact of Christianity on the continent.

For the most part, I believe the Christian experience in Africa had come largely through mass conversions into the Christian religion rather than real biblical discipleship that transformed the whole life. As a result, Africa has experienced a critical shortage of leaders both within and without the church, people who would live and lead as "the salt of the earth" and "the light of the world."[48]

The second question we considered had to do with the church's possible response to these challenges. We were convinced that many of Africa's problems could be solved if those of us who identify ourselves as Christians were living in obedience to the Word of God. This is so because the Bible teaches us to be men and women of character and integrity, to love our neighbors as we love ourselves, to promote peace and justice, and to care for the poor and the oppressed.

As D. Martin Lloyd-Jones of Wales argued in his book *The Cross*, "The ultimate answer to man's problems lies not in man, but in Jesus Christ."[49] Similarly, Oswald Chambers wrote in *My Utmost for His Highest*, "A man's disposition on the inside, i.e., what he possesses in his personality, determines what he is tempted by on the outside."[50]

We believed that God's message for Africans was the same as that which he spoke to the Israelites through the prophet Micah: "He has shown you, O mortal, what is good. And what does the Lord require of you? To act justly and to love mercy and to walk humbly with your God."[51]

We imagined what our churches, communities and societies would be like if love, mercy and justice were promoted and practiced in and through all of our life and relational networks.

The third question in our planning process examined expanding the vision beyond our organization, and strategies for doing so. Therefore, we asked, "How can we partner with churches and mission organizations?"

As a result, the vision grew from "our organization inviting others to join" to "the body of Christ working together for the glory of God." Accordingly, we started listing the names of influential individuals, church denominations, mission organizations, and even governmental and nongovernmental agencies who could partner in this endeavor.

The fourth question pointed us to strategies and resource mobilization. We listed both available strategies and potential ones. But more importantly, we agreed to empower people to be creative and to design strategies that were relevant in their context. As to the mobilization of material and financial resources, we developed a list of potential contributors (and contributing groups) both within Africa and elsewhere.

The average budget to reach a city was $160,000, for a total of $8 million. And we believed that most of the resources to reach a given city would be available within that same city. However, it would take leaders with conviction, passion and creativity to unearth those resources.

The fifth question led us to potential challenges and possible responses. The potential problems included persecution, inadequate financial resources, a shortage of leaders, lack of unity in the Christian community, poor planning, and lack of preparation to preserve and cultivate the fruit of the campaign.

The sixth question helped us clarify expectations and set standards of measurements. We approved the list of the 50 largest cities in the region, which were home to about 50 million people at the time. We also set some essential goals, including what to measure, significant activities, a timeline and quality control processes.

The seventh and the last question concerned possible organizational structures and division of responsibilities. Accordingly, we developed a structure that included major task forces such as project direction, prayer, fund development, operations, students, business, government, church mobilization and the media. However, we left the responsibilities of detailed planning and formation of task forces and ministry teams to the national and city leaders.

Through the group brainstorming process, we were able to gather the unique contributions of team members, create a shared vision, and visualize the magnitude and potential impact of the entire project. This process of group brainstorming — after which we developed and refined the plan — was repeated perhaps hundreds of times by teams and task forces in nations and cities across the region.

The most important stakeholders who needed to understand and own the vision before we went public with the project were our own staff members. Without that foundation, we could not implement the vision. So, in March 2000 we brought all the national leadership teams of our organization from

Southern and Eastern Africa to a meeting in Cyprus, where we shared the vision and involved them in the planning process.

Five months later, in August 2000, we invited all our staff members from the region to Nairobi, Kenya, to a gathering that God used to unite our hearts around the vision. The next critical step was to guide the body of Christ to also own the vision, to create the right organizational structure and lead its implementation.

Strategic Alliance

We knew that we needed a strategic alliance with partners, so we organized a regional vision and partnership conference in June 2001 in Nairobi. We invited 250 Christian leaders from the 23 countries. The list included heads of church denominations, mission CEOs, bishops, pastors, evangelists, business executives, senior government officials, lawyers, military officials, leaders from the media and national directors of our organization.

At the conference, I shared the overall vision and called for strategic alliance while Dela Adadevoh — serving at the time as a global vice president of our organization responsible for Africa, the Middle East and Central Asia — spoke on "Africa and the Impact of Christianity: Yesterday, Today and Tomorrow."[52]

Lazarus Seruyange, principal of Nairobi International School of Theology, also taught from the book of Malachi, emphasizing the conditions leading to revival as well as the results of revival. In his message, Seruyange highlighted one of the challenges facing the church in Africa: "We have weakened the message of the gospel. Easy salvation is preached, and people therefore receive the wrong message of coming to Christ and continuing in ancestral worship."

We presented a compelling vision. The participants deliberated in small groups on the content of the conference and answered five questions — questions designed to help participants not only understand, refine and own the vision but also commit themselves and their resources toward its fulfillment. What were the five questions?

1. What do you think of the vision? *A question of conviction*, necessary to create ownership of the vision.

2. How would you refine this vision? *A question of involvement*, necessary to give opportunities for leaders to shape the vision.

3. What potential challenges do you anticipate? *A question of problem-solving*, necessary to prepare leaders to solve problems in their cities.

4. What contributions can you and your organization make toward fulfilling this vision? *A question of commitment*, necessary to mobilize resources.

5. What critical next steps would you take in your country or city? *A question of action*, necessary to help leaders begin developing plans.

Through small group discussions and reflections at the plenary sessions, the participants suggested additional ideas and strategies, developed guiding principles for partnerships, identified possible challenges as well as preventive measures, and committed to mobilize necessary resources from their organizations and cities. Answering those five questions became a common practice in all the subsequent planning meetings in every country and city.

At the end of the conference, everyone felt a great excitement, unity and commitment to do whatever necessary to implement the vision in all the cities. In response, we created a powerful declaration — confirming our unity and commitment to work together — that was produced, read and approved at the conference.[53]

As the participants returned to their respective countries and cities, the same spirit, voice and energy echoed. The participants replicated the Nairobi vision and partnership conference in every country and city, casting the vision, establishing task forces and mobilizing workers. As a result, about 2,000 different task forces were established across the region with nearly 10,000 leaders involved in those task forces.

Questions and Doubts

As we prepared to implement that grand vision, not everything went smoothly. Some people questioned its credibility and scalability, as well as the motive behind the vision. But because we had already included possible questions and doubts on our list of expected challenges, we were not caught off guard. Here are some of the questions people raised, along with the answers we provided:

Question: Has God spoken?

Answer: Yes, God has spoken long ago, when he gave us the Great Commission in Matthew 28:19-20. Our best response is to obey the command.

Question: Is this not an unrealistic plan? How will this be possible?

Answer: This is not an unrealistic plan because Jesus said, "All things are possible with God" and, "Whoever believes in me will do the works I have been doing, and they will do even greater things than these." The Bible also says, "If we ask anything according to his will, he hears us."[54]

Question: Are the needed resources not too big to raise?

Answer: No, they are not too big to raise because, "The silver is mine and the gold is mine," declares the Lord Almighty," and, "The Lord will have men who will bring offerings in righteousness." We must believe in the nature and promises of God, as did Abraham, who knew that "what God had promised, he was able also to perform."[55]

Question: How can we get the commitment of churches?

Answer: Churches exist to fulfill the Great Commission, and all those who understand the purpose and the priority of the church will be involved. Our role is to share the vision, show how the churches can be involved, and provide necessary structure, tools and training.

Question: How can we ensure proper follow-up and discipleship?

Answer: Every task force will assume responsibility for answering this question; every plan and every training process must address the question of follow-up and discipleship.

Question: How can I be involved?

Answer: You can share the gospel with people who don't know Jesus. You can disciple new believers. You can pray. You can give financial and other material resources. You can receive training or train others. You can speak at Operation Sunrise events. You can be part of a task force. You can organize events. You can use your gifts, skills and profession to serve God and the people around you.

Big Vision, Small Pieces

Effective partnership strategies must be built around a common vision and mutual commitment, including:

- a commitment to work together regardless of denominational backgrounds and affiliations
- a willingness to share manpower, material, strategic and financial resources
- a desire to maintain pure motives and selflessness
- a willingness to seize opportunities for mutual growth and the furtherance of God's kingdom

In each city, a steering committee established at least 10 major task forces and hundreds of sub-task forces. Leaders and organizations with similar interests or emphases formed a task force and developed their own plans and budgets. For example, every church, mission agency or group that engaged in ministry among students in a given city came together and formed a student task force. The task force was responsible to develop and implement a strategic plan that included reaching every student in the city with the gospel, following up every student who would receive Christ, training and mobilizing every Christian student, and raising most of the necessary financial, material and strategy resources.

While giving the task forces freedom to be creative and contextually relevant, we still developed general guidelines. The guidelines included such things as job descriptions, measurement processes and management of partnership relationships.

Moreover, task forces organized vision and partnership conferences in their own areas of responsibility. Those conferences sought to clearly communicate the vision, define responsibilities, and develop the necessary manpower, material and financial resources. To help guide their planning process, task forces were given a template with 10 questions:

1. What are our responsibilities?

2. How do we accomplish our responsibilities?

3. How should we ensure the sustainability and long-term growth of the results?

4. What resources are available?

5. What additional resources do we need?

6. How should we mobilize the needed resources?

7. Who should do what?

8. What sub-task forces do we need to establish and why?

9. What is the timeline for each activity?

10. How do we measure our progress?

In each city, task force leaders reported to a city direction task force that, in turn, reported to a national direction task force. As director of the overall project, I wrote weekly updates to all partners, highlighting the significance of the task, sharing some of the great stories of God's work from across the region, and constantly motivating the workers.

A Visit With the President

After two years of planning and preparation, the campaign was launched on July 1, 2002, in 50 cities across Southern and Eastern Africa. To kick off the campaign, I traveled to Ethiopia and Kenya along with Steve Douglass (then international president of Campus Crusade) and a few business leaders from the United States.

While in Kenya, we visited the country's president at the Nakuru State House. Our group of 11 spent about an hour with President Daniel Toroitich arap

Moi and talked about our relationship with Jesus, the vision of Operation Sunrise, and the identity and mission of our organization. President Moi shared with us that he also loved Jesus, and one of his desires was to see Christians living in obedience to the Word of God and impacting their communities with righteousness.

While preparing for the visit, I read about Kenyan politics and learned that Kenyans were preparing for a national presidential election. Some Kenyans were questioning the integrity of President Moi, who had been in power for the previous 23 years. They were concerned he might run again for another term. As a result, the political environment in Kenya was getting tense.

Before leaving his office, I used the opportunity to offer the president my input. I believed he still had a lot to offer as a mentor but might best let younger, worthy leaders step up. So I said something like, "Your excellency, Mr. President, I know Kenyans will be electing their next president in December. Some newspapers have been reporting that you may be planning to run for another term. If at all possible, my humble suggestion for you would be *not* to run, but to be a good example to many young Africans as you have been so far."

The president replied, "Thank you for your input. I have heard you." After a word of prayer and posing for an official picture outside his office, we said goodbye. And five months later, in December 2002, Kenyans elected Mwai Kibaki as their new president and Daniel arap Moi made a peaceful transition out of office. Many African countries are still waiting for a day when presidents make peaceful transitions and mentor the next generation.

Later, regarding his experiences with Operation Sunrise, Steve Douglass commented, "It was one of the greatest experiences of my life. I saw men and women who loved God and displayed a burning passion to reach the lost in Africa. They shared a common sense of urgency and expectancy that God would fulfill the vision he imparted to them."

Questions for personal and group reflection

1. How was the brainstorming process that Bekele facilitated useful for his team to own the vision?

2. What principles have you learned about how to design and implement complex projects?

3. What are some important lessons you have learned in this chapter to effectively mobilize resources toward fulfilling a common vision?

4. Please respond: *In order to mobilize resources toward the vision God is giving me, I will* _____

   _____

   _____

   _____

Bekele and Shewa with Steve Douglass (second from right) and Dela Adadevoh during a staff conference for Southern and Eastern Africa held in Nairobi, Kenya, in August 2000

Bekele and Steve Douglass meet with Kenyan president Daniel arap Moi during Operation Sunrise in July 2002.

CHAPTER 10

Operation Sunrise Africa: Results

"The harvest is plentiful" (Matthew 9:37)

Some people may think Operation Sunrise just lasted 50 days. But it was much more. In reality, Operation Sunrise had three distinct phases. The first phase covered the two years that we spent developing and communicating the vision, mobilizing resources, and training task forces and volunteers. The second phase involved 50 days of momentum activities. And the third phase lasted three years after the campaign, with emphasis on follow-up and consolidation of the results.

During the campaign, about half a million Christians were trained and mobilized, and as mentioned earlier, 10,000 people helped give leadership to 2,000 task forces. Over 250 executive outreach dinners and luncheons were organized to reach professionals, diplomats, and business and government executives. Over 400 leaders from Africa and around the world participated as speakers at those events.

More than 2,000 people and multiple churches from outside Africa got involved,[56] including the United States, Canada, South Korea, Brazil, Hong Kong, Singapore, Australia and several European countries. The Jesus Film Project from the United States provided language translations, film prints, DVDs and equipment necessary to show the "JESUS" film.

We raised more than $8 million with about 70 percent raised locally from the cities. God promised the Israelites through the prophet Malachi, "The Lord will have men who will bring offerings in righteousness."[57] God fulfilled this promise to us as well. Generous partners, primarily from the United States, brought their financial offerings in righteousness and partnered with us in various cities.[58]

African American Students in Global Mission

At one point during our planning of Operation Sunrise, I had been invited to speak at a U.S. conference organized by The Impact Movement®, a ministry to African American college students. As I was preparing for this December 2000 event in Atlanta, Georgia, I felt led to invite all 1,500 of them to come to Africa during summer 2002 and get involved in Operation Sunrise. But I also knew finances might hinder their participation. I prayed about the idea and sensed the Holy Spirit was prompting me to challenge the students at the conference to make financial commitments.

I shared my thoughts with the conference leadership team. The team was not excited about the idea; they thought it would be difficult for the students to raise enough money for transportation to Africa, as well as accommodation. But out of their respect for me as a guest speaker from the "motherland," they let me go ahead with my plans. However, they warned me to be prepared for disappointment.

During my session, I spoke about Africa, what God was doing in the continent and the vision of Operation Sunrise. Then I challenged the students to come to Africa the summer of 2002. I also challenged them to give money at the conference. To our surprise, the students gave about $300,000 in cash and pledges. And many joined us in person and invited others. In the end, Impact would send a contingent of about 300 African Americans from across the country, including not only college students but also high school students, professionals and others.

At the end of Operation Sunrise, Charles Gilmer, national director of the Impact Movement at the time, wrote, "As far as we know, this is the largest mobilization of African Americans in an international mission effort in history! In this we rejoice. Indeed, we rejoice in the Lord and his great power and grace."

The Harvest Is Ripe

Operation Sunrise was the most complex multinational project I have ever led. This huge mobilization of the body of Christ took place in 50 cities, across 23 countries and over 50 days, with about 500,000 people being trained in ministry. More than 21,000 local churches and 300 international mission agencies worked together, raising $8 million.

Some national media outlets covered what we saw God doing. For example, in Tanzania, Christians offered to donate blood to the national blood bank. They requested television coverage and thus were able to declare live on TV: "We are donating blood to help save fellow Tanzanians. Those who will receive our blood may live for a few more years and then die. But there is Somebody who donated his blood for all humanity. Through his blood, we receive forgiveness of sins and eternal life. His name is Jesus. Today, we invite you to believe in Jesus and be saved from your sins."

The amazing campaign of the 50 days came to an end on August 19, 2002, and we started gathering reports. In almost every aspect we had surpassed our goals. For example, we had hoped to reach 50 million people with the gospel, but our follow-up reports totaled 64.5 million people, with 1.72 million people praying to invite Jesus into their life. Several cities not included in the original list of 50 joined the campaign, and our teams showed the "JESUS" film more than 8,000 times. In some of the cities, we saw decision rates ranging from 50 percent (in Zomba, Malawi) to 86 percent (in Eldoret, Kenya).[59] Truly, the harvest was ripe in Africa.

In addition to numerical results, we received hundreds of stories of faith and courage, sacrificial giving, leadership development, and the power of unity. Many lives were changed, and Christians became effective in sharing the gospel because they were trained.

"Why didn't you tell us that witnessing is so exciting?" said Palesa, a student in Lesotho. "No one, absolutely no one is going to stop me from going out and witnessing. I am going to my village and tell everyone about the Lord, it is so wonderful."

Similarly, a business executive in Tanzania commented, "Nobody has ever trained me on how to share my faith with others. I thank God for Operation Sunrise Africa."

Changed Lives

God did so many miracles through Operation Sunrise, and books could be written on what happened in each city. Trying to represent the numerous courageous exploits and thousands of stories in a single chapter in this book would not be a fair reflection. But telling a few is better than not telling any. . . .

Impatient Viewer

It appeared to be a typical "JESUS" film show in Zambia. Hundreds of people were gripped by the message before them, their eyes transfixed. Suddenly, a dark shadow fell across the screen, blocking the view. There was an uproar from the crowd when they realized it was a man standing in front of the projector. The "JESUS" film team members approached him, asking why he was disrupting the film. He exclaimed, "I have no time to wait for the film to finish, I want to receive Jesus Christ right now!" A staff member took him aside so the film could continue, and the man immediately placed his faith in Christ.

God's Rainstorm

Operation Sunrise Africa did not occur without opposition, which was greatest among local witch doctors. In Uganda, a radio advertisement called witch doctors from different areas to meet in order to conjure evil spirits against the strategy. They were to meet the following day in a large field to pronounce a curse. When the news came to Operation Sunrise staff members, they immediately met to pray against the gathering.

After a long night of prayer, the staff members awoke to the sounds of a tremendous rainstorm. It rained hard all day long, so hard that the witch doctors canceled their evening meeting.

Harvest Time

A church in Mombasa, Kenya, purchased 6,000 copies of the Four Spiritual Laws booklet, then leaders trained members during Sunday worship services to use this evangelism tool. One morning, the pastor told his congregation that he would not preach; instead, everyone should go into the city and tell people about Jesus Christ. After some time, the congregation came back to the church with news of more than 300 who had indicated decisions for Christ.

A Strong Man's Witness

A former member of Ethiopia's national army, Solomon Getachew, is a well-known boxer in his town of Dessie, Ethiopia. He works as a boxing trainer and competes in physical fitness and body-building activities. One night during Operation Sunrise, Getachew heard about the "JESUS" film showing in his area. He decided to attend and cause trouble.

He arrived halfway through the movie, but instead of being disruptive, Getachew was fascinated with the story on the screen before him. Forgetting his original intent, he watched the remainder of the film in silence. When it was finished, he asked the staff members if they would rewind the film, so he could see it from the beginning. They agreed to the big man's request, and that night Solomon Getachew invited Christ into his heart.

The next day, he went to his gym and excitedly invited all his friends and trainees to attend various "JESUS" film showings around the town. Since his conversion, Getachew has witnessed to over 100 people, with more than 50 coming to Christ.

Can't Be Ignored

On his way home from work, one man in Harare, Zimbabwe, stepped off the bus and noticed a group of people gathered near the bus stop. As he walked past, he saw that it was a "JESUS" film team just beginning to show the film. Ignoring it, he kept going toward home, only to find another "JESUS" film team just a few meters from his house. He could not ignore them this time and said, "These things are everywhere. I am confused. I don't know what is happening." He watched the film and afterward prayed to receive Christ.

From Ushiazase to Zola

Soweto is one of the largest townships near Johannesburg, South Africa, with an estimated 4 to 5 million people, setting the trend for many things that happen in other black townships. One famous suburb had the Zulu name *Ushiazase*, which means, "beat him until he dies." Any time people in this place fought, no one would intervene — they would fight until somebody died. The pastors of Ushiazase began praying together, asking God to transform the area to a place of peace.

They prayed and shared the gospel throughout the community, and now that suburb carries a new name, *Zola,* the Zulu word for "peace." Anyone can go into Zola today without fear because the gospel has brought transformation.

The Adventure Is Not Yet Over

By the time we concluded Operation Sunrise, my family and I had been in Zimbabwe for three years. The campaign was over, but my life would never be the same. I had experienced God in a new way and seen him do the impossible. God smiles when we ask him for big things because he is a big God. When our plan is too small, we limit what God can do through us.

I have also learned about the extraordinary power that exists in unity and partnerships. When we come together to fulfill a common vision that aligns with God's will, there is no mountain too high to climb, no challenge too big to overcome and no plan too complex to implement. God is pleased with the unity of his children and he blesses the work of their hands.

The vital experiences I gained through Operation Sunrise would become additional steppingstones to the destiny God had prepared for me.

Questions for personal and group reflection

1. Where and how is the harvest plentiful in the world today?

2. As you read about Operation Sunrise Africa, what did you observe regarding God's faithfulness to honor the faith of his servants?

3. What are some of your own experiences in trusting God for something big?

4. Please respond: *One thing God might be calling me to do, right now, toward the growth of his kingdom is* _____

_____

_____

_____

CHAPTER 11

Career Conflict

"Many are the plans in a person's heart, but it is the Lord's purpose that prevails" (Proverbs 19:21)

The final days of Operation Sunrise launched us into the second half of our six years in Zimbabwe. The country was beginning a descent into political and economic distress, and at the same time, so was my family and team. As a team, we faced incredible challenges that forced us to relocate our regional office to Pretoria, South Africa.

Yet my family and I experienced some of the greatest blessings from God, as well as challenges, during those eight years after Operation Sunrise — three in Zimbabwe and five in South Africa.

Leaving Zimbabwe

Due to the land redistribution policy — which lacked proper planning and wise implementation by the government — the Zimbabwean national economy dramatically collapsed and the country suffered serious consequences. When my family and I had arrived in Zimbabwe in 1999, 10 Zimbabwean dollars equaled about one American dollar. But not long after Operation Sunrise, and seemingly overnight, the exchange rate plummeted to about 3 trillion Zimbabwean dollars to the American dollar.

The national bank tried to cope with the hyperinflation by frequently and progressively introducing new banknotes for thousands, millions, billions and then trillions of dollars. People would commonly go to coffee shops carrying money in backpacks.

Scarcity of essential commodities such as bread, sugar, salt, milk and soap hit the whole country. Formal and informal traders brought commodities from neighboring countries such as South Africa, Botswana and Zambia and sold them at triple the normal price. Long queues formed outside grocery stores and banks. And at gas stations, people stayed overnight in their vehicles, hoping to find gas the next day. As it was difficult to maintain a failed system, the bank finally discontinued the printing of more money and introduced the use of foreign currencies such as the American dollar, the British pound or the South African rand.

The banks also issued a daily limit on how much money a person or a company could withdraw from their own bank accounts, a situation that affected our ministry. For example, whenever we organized a conference in Harare, we were required to submit the budget of the conference — including names of participants — and get approval from the central bank to use our own money. It became clear that we could not sustain our ministry operation in that situation, so in 2005 we relocated the regional office to Pretoria, South Africa.

Sustainable Ministry Results

From 2003 to 2007, we sought to build on the gains made through Operation Sunrise. Yet as we evaluated the effectiveness of our ministries in the region, we discovered some critical weaknesses:

First, through our campus ministries, we were presenting the gospel to students and making disciples on college campuses, but we lacked clear processes on how to maintain our relationship with the students after graduation and involve them in ministry.

Second, we had over 300 "JESUS" film teams in the region. Almost all were funded from the United States, complete with ministry requirements. For example, each team was required to show the film 100 times a year, expose about 30,000 people to the gospel and expect salvation decisions from about 10 percent of viewers. Those requirements kept them so busy, the teams didn't have enough time to disciple new believers, build relationships with local pastors, or train existing Christians in evangelism and discipleship. We realized that we were contributing to the spiritual shallowness of the church in Africa.

Third, the various departments within our organization were acting as independent ministries and competing for resources instead of collaborating and optimizing resources.

These and other related challenges led us to start a strategy we called "Expansion Movement." This decision turned out to be one of the most important moves we made as a team. Through this strategy, we sought to:

- keep college graduates involved in ministry for the long term
- strengthen discipleship
- use the "JESUS" film as a church-planting strategy
- build relationships with leaders of various church denominations and use those relationships to mobilize Christians for the Great Commission

Most importantly, perhaps, Expansion Movement enabled our ministry teams to cooperate with one another and maximize the use of resources. For example, college students helped show the "JESUS" film and plant churches. Marketplace leaders provided resources to campus ministries as well as church planters. Churches prepared high-school graduates to launch student ministries when they went to college.

However, our decision to create a new ministry department around this strategy had consequences. First, this department did not exist in our global organization. Second, using the "JESUS" film as a church-planting strategy would force us to say no to some of the requirements of the Jesus Film Project office in the United States. Instead of each team showing the film 100 times a year, they would spend time building relationships with local pastors, training believers, planting churches and mentoring leaders of the new churches.

For that to happen, we needed to engage the global leadership of the Jesus Film Project in a change process and create mutual understanding. The process also included educating donors on why the number of "JESUS" film showings and gospel exposures would be lower than in the past.

The leaders of our organization elsewhere in the world took notice of the work we were doing. Thus, within a year or two, the regions of West Africa, Francophone Africa, North Africa and the Middle East, and Central Asia also decided to launch Expansion Movement, a department that added effectiveness to what they were doing.

Apartheid's Evils

South Africa was an intriguing country, with 11 national languages, three different capital cities and the fifth-largest population in Africa. As the industrial powerhouse of the continent, it was a melting pot of modernity and tradition. People of various geographic origins lived in distinct settlements, though the situation had been gradually changing since the fall of apartheid in the early 1990s. Nevertheless, wounds from the repressive apartheid regime still ran deep and felt fresh.

By spending a few hours at the Apartheid Museum in Johannesburg and Robben Island near Cape Town (where Nelson Mandela was jailed for years), we learned a lot more about the evil of apartheid. The 1913 Land Act, which created racial segregation and white domination, forced black Africans out of their ancestral lands and into reserves. Just visiting one of these two sites is enough to expose the darkness of the human heart.

Slave traders brought poor people to South Africa from as far away as Malaysia, Madagascar and Indonesia. A few white European settlers who arrived in Cape Town in 1652 attracted their kith and kin, gradually increased in numbers and took over about 92 percent of the native land. Consequently, black Africans were robbed of their material assets and precious freedom, then victimized and humiliated in their own country.

But through the sacrifices of many South Africans as well as pressure from the international community, the light of freedom shone. Many know of activists Nelson Mandela and Steven Biko. But there's also Solomon Mahlangu, a black South African who cried out just before his execution in 1979: "My blood will nourish the tree which will bear fruits of freedom. Tell my people that I love them and that they must continue the struggle. Do not worry about me but about those who are suffering."[60]

When I read that and other similar statements in one of history's darkest museums, I prayed for South Africa. I prayed that the ideals of freedom, equality and responsibility would never be eroded, nor be replaced by selfishness, greed, crime and corruption. And I pray that the unconditional forgiveness and racial reconciliation that Mr. Mandela preached after his release from prison and during his presidency will continue to characterize that colorful rainbow nation.

Honest and Competent Leaders

During my leadership in the region, I came face to face with the critical shortage of authentic servant-leaders — people of integrity who were both self-aware and fully capable in their role. I witnessed this lacking both in the church and in society in general.

For example, I helped coordinate the transitions of 30 national leaders during my decade of leadership in Southern and Eastern Africa. Twenty of those transitions were difficult and painful due to abuse of power, misappropriation of resources or unhealthy relationships. Yet I also identified lack of intentional training and preparation as a primary cause for leadership failure.

As a result, I initiated the Emerging Leaders Initiative: a two-year, intensive, transformational process that focused on character formation and authentic leadership. After developing ELI in 2007, we launched our first cohort with 24 students selected from nine countries in the region.

The program focused on younger leaders, ages 25 to 35. The teaching-learning processes included exposure to best practices from other organizations as well as group debates, peer-mentoring, formal and informal coaching, and opportunities to lead national and international projects.

More than a decade later, as I write this page, we have graduated six cohorts of students, many of whom now lead at the national, continental and global levels of Campus Crusade. And what used to be ELI in Africa has now become the Global Academy for Transformational Leadership and offers an accredited M.A. degree in transformational leadership.

GATL attracts the interest of many younger leaders from around the world. Through GATL, they develop their own personal constitution, identify core values, create a personal mission statement and grow in self-awareness.

In addition, GATL encourages students to view stewardship from the perspectives of self, people, mission and resources. The training is available at their locations and while on the job, so students do not need to travel far, leave their responsibilities or pay excessive amounts of money. GATL is not only mobile, cost-effective, practical and globally available, but it also equips younger leaders to become God-dependent, confident, strategic and entrepreneurial.

Launching Pamoja Africa

In 2003, the West Africa office of our organization invited me to speak at a Christmas conference for students known as Destiny West Africa. A total of 513 college students and young professionals came from several countries in West Africa, including Nigeria, Ghana, Liberia and Sierra Leone.

Before concluding the conference, I suggested to Ben Ecklu, my counterpart in West Africa at the time and now with the Lord, the possibility of growing the conference beyond West Africa and making it a continental strategy of convening, inspiring and cultivating next-generation leaders.

Ben was a dear friend whom I had known for more than 12 years. Together with many other African leaders, Ben and I shared a similar vision: to see Christianity play a major role in the holistic transformation of Africa and its spiritual, cultural, political and socioeconomic life. He was a humble servant of the Lord who cared deeply for people and maintained a wholehearted commitment to see the development of Christ-centered transformational leaders for the continent.

At the conclusion of Destiny West Africa, Ben and I announced that we would organize a series of all-Africa conferences for students and young professionals, with the first taking place in three years. We envisioned these conferences as catalysts for developing leaders — leaders who would help accelerate global evangelization and fight some of Africa's chronic socioeconomic problems. We set up a continental leadership team and coined "Pamoja Africa" as the name of the conference. *Pamoja*, a KiSwahili word, means "together."

Since 2006, Pamoja Africa conferences have now been held roughly every three years and include pastors, church planters and leaders of church denominations. We help participants develop a vision for a new Africa in which people understand and practice the virtues of peace, love, integrity, justice, equality and prosperity, which come from knowing and obeying the gospel of Jesus Christ. In addition, Pamoja Africa creates one of the few opportunities for young leaders from the whole continent to come together and learn about God's plan for their continent and the world.

A Growing Restlessness

In 2004, I enrolled in Operation Impact, a popular program by Azusa Pacific University in Southern California that offered an M.A. degree in organizational leadership. The courses were practical, offered as one-week modules and available in many locations around the world. Since I wanted to learn more about the political environment in Ethiopia, I decided to take the courses together with some of the top government leaders there.

I spent six weeks with about 100 Ethiopian politicians and gained significant insight into their personalities, abilities and the challenges they were facing. Through that, I learned that basic leadership concepts such as mentoring and servant leadership were new to some of them.

This experience also helped me realize the shortcomings of education in Ethiopia. For example, one of the greatest socioeconomic challenges Ethiopia has traditionally faced is poverty, yet schools then, as well as now, produce few graduates who knew how to tackle the problem. Most of the political leaders I met during the Azusa Pacific courses were college graduates with degrees in engineering, biology, chemistry and so on, but not in governance, public policy or public leadership. If education were relevant in Ethiopia — and in Africa — our schools would be producing hundreds and thousands of graduates who know how to develop Africa's extraordinary natural resources and overcome poverty.

While in Ethiopia for the courses, I toured various areas of the country, excited to check out new developments. However, I repeatedly heard comments such as "not allowed," "impossible" and "you cannot do this." Even to this day, it is more common in Ethiopia to hear "you cannot" than "you can."

For example, I tried to visit Hawassa University, one of the newly established public universities. But when my driver and I arrived at the university gate, the security officer told us, "You are not allowed to drive your car to the campus, you have to walk." We tried to convince the guard that it was quite a distance and inconvenient, but he would not let us in. When we left the place, I was discouraged.

Then I asked my driver what else was new in the city. He told me that the city's first-ever hospital was being built. I asked him to take me there. We arrived at the construction site only to be told, "Entry to the construction site is impossible."

I wonder what would be different all across Ethiopia and among its emerging leaders if we used empowering and encouraging phrases such as, "you can do it, it's possible, try, be bold, make a mistake and learn from it"?

I began to sense a growing internal restlessness and hunger related to so much of my previous years' experience. I wanted to do more to positively influence my generation. I wanted to contribute toward Africa's holistic development. I wanted to see the church of Jesus Christ becoming more relevant in the daily life of an African man or woman. I wanted to see churches preaching the gospel that addresses spiritual, social, physical, mental and financial needs.

These varied passions and desires would lead me to an array of conflicting career choices over the next few years. Yet God would use the courses I was taking and the Azusa Pacific University professors to help me navigate that journey.[61]

Future Career Options

In 2004, at age 36, I decided to take three months to learn about myself, listen to my heart and seek God's guidance about the many things I wanted to do in order to help people in Ethiopia, Africa and the world. I listed all the important things burdening my heart and narrowed them down to only four.

First, there was the option of joining politics in Ethiopia — a desire that had been growing as I saw the endless sufferings of my fellow Ethiopians: material poverty, massive unemployment, poor quality of education, underdeveloped natural resources, government policies that hindered creativity and entrepreneurial spirit, and the like. Several senior government officials, as well as church leaders, frequently said to me: "This country needs you. Please come and help." I took their invitation seriously and kept it as one of my top four career options.

Second, I wanted to establish a university for Africa that would address the critical need for informed and competent leaders. To that end, I took time to develop a vision for the university that included four schools: a school of public leadership, a school of business and economic leadership, a school of educational leadership, and a school of church leadership.

The university would be located in Addis Ababa; it would partner with the African Union (headquartered in the same city); and it would focus on training the brightest students from all over Africa. As I shared the vision with friends, professors and government officials, I received encouraging feedback. I even created an organizational structure and named a global board for the school.

Third, I desired to plant and lead a megachurch in Addis Ababa. I envisioned a community of believers that would inspire and equip people to be the salt of the earth and the light of the world. As teaching hospitals produce doctors for all other hospitals, I wanted this church to produce godly and competent leaders for other churches in the country. I desired to have a church that would show compassion for the poor and the marginalized and preach a gospel that integrates the spiritual and the physical. I wanted a model church that would preach the gospel, make disciples, train leaders, send missionaries abroad, establish universities and hospitals, and care for the poor and the oppressed.

Fourth, I kept open the option of continuing what I had been doing in and through our organization for the previous 10 years.

During this journey of intensive soul-searching, I worked through self-assessment tests — reading and reflecting on the Word of God and other relevant books, and evaluating the pros and cons of each career option. I developed a 25-page personal constitution that included my core values, the highlights of my strengths and weaknesses, my personal mission statement, my leadership philosophy, and my long-term personal development goals.

I identified *service*, *excellence* and *influence* as my core values — the core of who I am and the guiding principles of my life. Through the value of *service*, I seek to serve the purpose of God in my generation and add value to people. The value of *excellence* motivates me to be and do my best with a sense of urgency and dedication. And through the value of *influence*, I live to help one person at a time, positively influence my generation and leave a lasting legacy.

Moreover, the mission statement gave me a clear direction as to which way to go: "*I exist to serve the purpose of God in my generation by empowering the body of Christ for world evangelization that results in holistic transformation of humanity.*"

Through that process, I realized that my scope was the whole world — not just Ethiopia or Africa; my niche was the body of Christ; and my sense of fulfillment came from helping people know God and experience his plan of salvation.

The whole process took three months, after which the gracious Lord guided me to choose the fourth option, which was to stay in Campus Crusade. Still, deep down in my heart, I knew God was preparing me for something bigger and more exciting.

Questions for personal and group reflection

1. What do you learn from Bekele's experiences of using challenges as opportunities?

2. Have you ever experienced career conflict in your life? How did you resolve it?

3. Have you articulated your personal core values and mission statement? What are they, and how do you live them out on a daily basis?

4. Please respond: *One step I will take to implement what I've read in this chapter is* _____

   _____

   _____

   _____

CHAPTER 12

A 100-Year Vision for Ethiopia

"Write the vision; make it plain on tablets" (Habbakuk 2:2)

S oon after the excitement of Operation Sunrise Africa and the resolution of my career conflicts, Shewa was diagnosed with a blockage of the right ureter, the tube that carries urine from the kidney to the bladder. She eventually had surgery in Zimbabwe in May 2005.

The doctor was a believer and highly respected. However, we did not know the extent to which health facilities in Zimbabwe lacked medical supplies. The doctor expected to discharge her from the hospital after a week, but Shewa did not improve and could not be discharged even after eight weeks.

In July 2005, two months after her surgery, we decided to airlift her to Pretoria East Hospital in South Africa. By the time we arrived, she was very weak. After a series of medical tests, the doctors confirmed that she needed additional treatments and weeks of antibiotics.

We were told later that a faulty stent used on the day of surgery in Zimbabwe (due to a shortage of proper stents) was to blame for all the complications. And God protected her from a second surgery that had been planned in Zimbabwe — a surgery that would have made things even worse. The slow journey to recovery in South Africa would take four years.

We experienced so much encouragement and so many miracles during that time of suffering. Friends and colleagues around the world overwhelmingly supported us in prayer. Hundreds of emails, phone calls, letters and cards poured in. We were never alone.

At the end of the first week at Pretoria East Hospital, the doctor told us that we must stay in South Africa for the next six months for follow-up. Due to the office relocation mentioned earlier, we had already secured work permits for South Africa. So my next step was to work on our family's move from Zimbabwe.

Since Shewa was still in the hospital, I needed to coordinate the move by myself: saying goodbye to friends, selling our possessions and bringing the children to South Africa, where we would need a new house, vehicles and furniture.

In her hospital room, Shewa and I asked God for the miracles needed. We then watched God provide a home within a few days (just in time for Shewa to move in straight from the hospital), a bank loan in South Africa despite no credit history there and amazing friends to come alongside for the move.[62]

Once back in Zimbabwe, I gave myself less than a week to sell the house, cars and furniture, buy airline tickets, ship some of the most important items, and bring our children to South Africa.[63] Then, on August 5, 2005, I flew to South Africa with the kids, moved straight into our new house and reunited with my wife.

God was answering all our prayers: Shewa was making significant improvement, the shipment from Zimbabwe arrived in just six days, and our children enrolled at Hatfield Christian School.

During Shewa's four years of recovery, 2004 to 2008, we experienced another miracle: Her body, which had been enfeebled by medication and frequent invasions to insert and remove stents, was able to carry and deliver our precious fourth child on February 12, 2007. The doctors could not believe that Shewa had no medical complications during her pregnancy. Hence, we named our baby girl Nes-El, meaning, "miracle of God." The name eventually evolved into Nesiel, and we nicknamed her Nessy.

God has truly answered the prayers of many friends. We have experienced the words Paul wrote to the believers at Corinth: "We are hard pressed on every side, but not crushed; perplexed, but not in despair; persecuted, but not abandoned; struck down, but not destroyed."[64]

So we sang with the Psalmist, "Give thanks to the Lord, for he is good; his love endures forever. . . . When hard pressed, I cried to the Lord; he brought me into a spacious place. . . . The Lord is with me; he is my helper. I look in triumph on my enemies."[65]

Ethiopia's Paradox

I thought I had resolved my career conflict back in 2004. Not fully true, it turned out. I still found myself carrying the burden of helping my home country, Ethiopia. This time, though, it was not about joining politics but helping the church play a key role in the area of holistic national development. I had tried to forget about the church in Ethiopia and focus on my role in Southern and Eastern Africa, but the burden simply would not go away.

Though Ethiopia had been a Christian nation for almost 2,000 years, it still had one of the lowest incomes of any nation on Earth. The church lacked strategic vision and systematic development, coordination and utilization of resources. Due to limited education and training, the incredible human resource potential was largely untapped. And due to inadequate discipleship, Christianity had not yet made a real impact on the socioeconomic, political and cultural life of the nation.

After being saved from their sins through the gospel of Jesus, many Ethiopian and African Christians had not been taught the whole counsel of the Bible that teaches us to care for orphans and widows, to steward God's creation around us, and to be the light of the world and the salt of the earth.[66] Despite the many Christians in Ethiopia, the nation was overwhelmed with unprecedented social and economic challenges such as poverty, illiteracy, environmental degradation, brain-drain, poor governance, rampant corruption, ethnic violence and civil unrest.

Moreover, the leadership potential of women was extremely underdeveloped. Although more than 60 percent of the nation's population claimed to be Christian, the church had not yet developed the necessary theological framework and spiritual voice to uphold and advocate biblical values of love and peace, freedom and equality, justice and the sanctity of life, environmental stewardship, and the rights of women and children.

The Ethiopian church, considered by some in 1998 to be one of the fastest-growing in the world,[67] faced a massive shortage of leaders, Bible teachers, trained pastors, theologians and strategists. The church's inability to develop and implement a clear, long-term, holistic vision had contributed to the nation's problems. The average Ethiopian Christian didn't know how to apply his or her Christian faith to the issues of daily life.

For instance, the living conditions of the people in the village in which I was born had remained virtually the same for the past four decades. During that same period, the population probably tripled, but the main food source remained the same: local people using a primitive way of farming with oxen. Yet in the area where I was born, nearly 95 percent of the people follow Jesus. But what did Jesus teach? Did he only teach about salvation of the soul? Or did he also heal the sick, care for the poor, and give dignity and freedom to individuals and families?

And what did Jesus mean when he told us, "You are the salt of the earth. . . . You are the light of the world?"[68] Shouldn't his teachings also empower obedient Christians to make a difference in their lives and the lives of others around them?

With this burden, I traveled from South Africa to Ethiopia and brought together 11 influential Ethiopian Christian leaders in March 2006. I told them I would like us to organize a national congress for Christian leaders from all spheres of life: church, government, media, business, education, etc. — and help develop a 100-year strategic vision for the country from a biblical perspective.

The leaders asked if I had any success story or example from around the world that I could share with them. "Not at this moment," I replied. I remembered an advertisement I had seen on a billboard in South Africa: "Do not follow where the path may lead, go instead where there is no path and leave a trail."

So I told the leaders, "I don't have any example of a 100-year strategic vision to share with you, but we can create one." I presented my initial ideas and what we needed to do:

- organize a congress on holistic national development

- identify critical national issues

- select people to research those topics using a common template, then present papers at the congress

- invite each presenter to propose a maximum of five strategic ideas that would inform our long-term vision

- carefully select and invite participants, including Christian leaders from the church, government, media, business and other professions.

The team embraced my ideas. We prayed together and started working right away. We identified 17 topics of national concern, including national evangelization, in-depth discipleship, unity and collaboration in the body of Christ, national economic development, environmental stewardship, development of children and youth, empowerment of women, leadership development and mobilizing the Ethiopian church for global mission. Then we identified people to research those topics and prepare presentations.

Developing a Plan

Six months later, in October 2006, we held our first national congress in Sodere, a resort area about 70 miles southeast of Addis Ababa. A total of 165 Christian leaders attended, presenting 17 papers recommending 80 different strategies. In small groups, the participants discussed each paper and made significant improvements to the strategies. At the end of the congress, we formed 12 task forces (condensed from the original 17) to continue working on the long-term vision and agreed to organize a second congress after nine months. But between the first and the second congress, all the planning teams came together to share and critique one another's initial plans.

Then we organized a second congress in July 2007 in Hawassa, capital of Southern Ethiopia. This time, 168 leaders attended. The 12 task forces presented their draft strategic plans, which participants critically evaluated. The essential components of the plans included such elements as advocacy and peacebuilding; national evangelization; development of children, youth and women; economic development; environmental development and protection; and media and communication.

The final congress took place in October 2007 in Addis Ababa. Its objective was to unveil the national strategic vision. In addition to over 500 Ethiopian Christian leaders, we had invited leaders from 24 African countries and beyond to witness the potential of the church in advancing holistic national transformation from a biblical perspective. With great excitement and a sense of fulfillment, we unveiled the vision. The vision document included goals like:

- train 400,000 leaders
- plant 31,000 additional churches
- engage all 29 unengaged and unreached people groups with the gospel
- work in partnership with the government to plant 500 million trees
- develop a national center for research and missions
- establish Christian foundations and charities

Together, we promoted Bible-based holistic transformation and leadership development. We longed to see Ethiopians experience freedom from the power of sin and oppressive socioeconomic conditions. We desired to see multiplication of leaders of character and competence. We aimed at promoting creative development and effective management of resources. We hoped to see the church of Jesus Christ become a beacon of hope, a spring of life, a place of love and a source of excellence.

To capture the spirit of that 100-year vision, we coined the term Ethiopia National Excellence Center. We established a national board and set up an operational team to guide the ENEC's implementation. Then we presented the vision to key government leaders. They were surprised and excited to see that the church was concerned about national development and able to develop a long-term vision. They told us, "If what you are telling us is true, then the church in Ethiopia has matured."

Next they asked: "How can the government partner with you?"

At the end of the presentation and discussions, a personal adviser to the late Prime Minister Meles Zenawi approached me and said, "Bekele, I really appreciated what I have heard tonight. This is what the government needs. As a government, we don't have a long-term plan. Would you give me your PowerPoint presentation and a copy of your book so that I could present them to our prime minister?"

I cannot be sure it was inspired by our group's 100-year vision, but a few months later the Ethiopian government unveiled a five-year national transformation plan.

Nevertheless, while the tears of joy were still warm on our cheeks, our own vision faced a huge challenge: "Under whose authority should this vision fall?" Some asked this question from a genuine desire to see the fulfillment of the vision, while others asked from a desire to be in charge. Various suggestions arose, and at one point in time we had 12 options as to whose umbrella the Ethiopia National Excellence Center should fall under. We got stuck.

Have I Finished My Role?

At that time, my family and I were living in South Africa, and I had no space in my busy schedule to help facilitate the implementation of ENEC in Ethiopia. Even had I wanted to, I could not have given even 5 percent of my time. But some good friends in Ethiopia were asking me to return to my home country and lead the implementation. Of course, I did not want to see that glorious vision decline and die. Shewa and I wanted to know what to do, so we cried out to God. We considered moving back to Ethiopia. At one point, we even looked at housing and schools for our children in Addis Ababa.

Once more I was at a crossroads. Was it the right time for me to leave my role in Campus Crusade for Christ? Should we continue living in Constantia Park, a beautiful suburb in eastern Pretoria, or move back to Ethiopia, a place where basic internet connection was a nightmare? I was caught between keeping my commitment to our organization and saving the vision in Ethiopia. We were desperate to hear the voice of God and to know which way to go.

Then on February 13, 2010, about 28 months after we unveiled the vision of ENEC, a phone call came from America that answered our earnest prayer. "Bekele, we have been working on organizational restructuring," Steve Douglass said. "We are starting a new global department that would focus on resourcing and planting churches worldwide. We have been praying for a leader for this role. Would you be interested in guiding the establishment of this new department?"

I asked Steve to give us about two weeks to pray, and then Shewa and I asked God for his guidance. The Lord reminded me of the personal mission statement I had developed six years earlier: "I exist to serve the purpose of God in my generation by empowering the body of Christ for world evangelization that results in holistic transformation of humanity."

In the mission statement, I noticed the phrases "the body of Christ" and "world evangelization." It was like, "Wow, God had already given me a clear direction!" I told Steve Douglass that we would be honored to accept the role.

The lack of full implementation of the ENEC vision in Ethiopia deeply pained me,[69] but the dilemma had passed. We were beginning a new chapter, with a new team to form, a new department to establish, a global role to assume, a move to America, and a new people and culture to learn about. And we were taking with us God's promise: "I am with you always."[70]

Questions for personal and group reflection

1. Can you think of one significant challenge you have faced in your life or a vision that has never been fulfilled? What leadership lessons have you learned through them?

2. What leadership-development processes do you have in place for your ministry or church?

3. What leadership lesson(s) did you learn from the billboard ad from South Africa: "Do not follow where the path may lead, go instead where there is no path and leave a trail"?

4. Please respond: *One step I will take to implement what I've read in this chapter is* _____

   _____

   _____

   _____

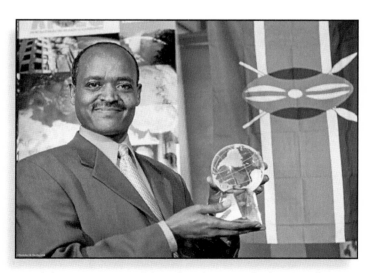

Bekele receives an award from the African Leadership Foundation.

CHAPTER 13

The Beautiful Body of Christ

*"Now you are the body of Christ, and each one of you
is a part of it" (1 Corinthians 12:27)*

Exactly two years before my new global role, I had traveled to Accra, Ghana,
with a group of international students for a doctoral course with Bakke
Graduate University. Near the end of the course, God deepened my understanding
of the church of Jesus Christ on a day I will remember for a lifetime — a day spent
visiting and learning from a cross-section of churches in Accra; a day in which
we were masterfully exposed to the diversity and beauty of the body of Christ.

Dr. Ray Bakke, theologian and course instructor, had spoken several times
on a defining moment in his life, when Billy Graham counseled him, "Never divide
the body of Christ." That simple but profound advice had impacted his spiritual
life and relationships with churches. That truth echoed through my mind as we
visited nine different churches that day.

Regardless of size, location, history, or ministry strategy and practice,
every local church or denomination is God's gift to this world. Every church that
confesses "Jesus is Lord" is a member of the body of Christ and belongs to Jesus,
who is its owner, head, shepherd and master.

The churches we visited varied in size from True Christian Church, with
about 25 people gathered in a small, rented classroom, to Lighthouse Chapel

International, with a splendid facility and at the time more than 500 branches worldwide. The churches also varied in other ways:

- In some, worshippers enjoyed contemporary music with dancing and loud drums, while in others, they sang contemplative hymns.

- Some churches had expensive seats — others, dusty benches.

- Some churches owned gothic-style buildings, while others used small, rented facilities.

- Some churches had established educational institutions, while others struggled financially.

- Some churches were nearly two centuries old — others, newly established.

- Some churches reinvented themselves to attract the younger generation, while others kept their status quo.

- Some had expanded community development programs, while others emphasized caring for their own members.

But what was common to all of them? As I observed from their vision and mission statements, all the churches existed to glorify God. To achieve this, they sought to remain faithful to the Word of God, take the gospel to the nations, make disciples, train believers for ministry, confront evil, and care for the poor as well as the environment. Each made a unique contribution toward building the eternal kingdom of God.

While facilitating the course, Dr. Bakke commented, "We cannot find one church that meets all the needs of this world." Instead, we need each other and must appreciate and celebrate our specific gifts and contributions. As the apostle Paul said, "If one part suffers, every part suffers with it; if one part is honored, every part rejoices with it."[71]

Local Church, Global Powerhouse

I found the physical infrastructure of Lighthouse Chapel International impressive, as well as the scope and diversity of its ministry. Yet I also believe it's one of the best examples on the continent of how a local church can have a global impact. I learned several specific things from that particular church:

First, Africa has enough resources to do the work of God, but the church needs a clear vision and strategy to mobilize those resources. Ghanaian Christians built not only Lighthouse Chapel International but also its international branches.

Second, there is no limit to what a person can do under God's leading and empowerment. Bishop Dag Heward-Mills, who started the chapel in 1987 as a ministry to medical students, has seen hundreds of churches planted and thousands of trained lay people involved in ministry nationally and internationally. In fact, the network of churches arising from Lighthouse Christian Chapel has grown to include 6,075 branches in 92 countries.

Third, there is power in training and sending people. One of this church's greatest strengths has been to empower its members to carry out the vision wherever they go and live.

However, even while praising God for the many great things happening in Accra through the churches, I was also concerned about a few things.

First, we saw four different churches in one location, and some churches side by side, concentrating the light of the kingdom in one place and competing with one another — rather than distributing the light of the kingdom so that it shines in every dark corner.

Second, the church was unable to address some critical social and economic problems due to the lack of unity in the body of Christ and the lack of a collective national vision. For instance, Accra is home to a horrific slum called by its nickname Sodom and Gomorrah, where the world's digital waste is sorted and burned for traces of valuable materials. How are the churches in the city having an impact there?

Through that wonderful exposure to different churches, God opened my eyes to see one universal and eternal church — the bride of Jesus Christ — beyond the logos, names, sizes and affiliations that tend to divide us. Of course, we will continue to have many logos and names until the day the bride meets her Bridegroom. Every church has a specific contribution to make and must be appreciated and supported by the rest of the body of Christ. These are critical and foundational elements for healthy collaboration.

A Church-Planting Framework

The first important step in my new role was to identify several Campus Crusade staff members from around the world who had experience in planting churches within the context of our organization and invite them to Pretoria, South Africa, to develop a framework.

Accordingly, 16 people attended a three-day prayer and planning consultation in our office in May 2010.[72] We sought to accomplish three objectives:

First, we wanted to hear from each other and learn what God was already doing around the world in and through our organization in relation to church planting.

Second, I wanted the group to develop a framework for our global department that regions and countries could use as a guide to develop their own vision, strategies and processes.

Third, I had a hidden agenda of recruiting some of them to join my team.

In preparation to the consultation, I created 12 questions for group brainstorming, including:

- What is our mission statement?

- What would be our core contributions?

- What is our working description of a church?

- What are our key strategies?

- How do we collaborate in the body of Christ?

- How might church planting look like in various social, demographic and religious contexts?

I divided the group into two teams and gave each a set of six questions. Each team worked on two questions a day and presented the outcome of their work in the afternoons. The whole group then provided input. The process was repeated over the three days, and at the end we had our initial framework for what would become Global Church Movements.

We also identified five core contributions that GCM could make toward accelerating global evangelization through church-multiplication movements. Regardless of culture, church tradition or the level of evangelization, we could apply those five core contributions anywhere:

First, as GCM, we can *inspire vision and action* toward the fulfillment of the Great Commission through evangelism, discipleship and church multiplication. The church of Jesus Christ needs to realize that:

- Every person on the planet deserves to hear the good news of our Lord Jesus Christ.

- Every Christian is expected to be a disciple of Jesus and disciple others.

- Every church is a center for local and global mission.

- The primary role of every pastor is to equip the saints for ministry.

- Every workplace a Christian man or woman occupies is a mission field and an assignment from God.

- Every church is expected to plant multiplying churches that show and tell the love and the goodness of God.

Second, we can *train multiplying missional leaders* toward the fulfillment of the Great Commission. This emphasis would enable us to equip leaders who are aligned with God's heart for both the Great Commandment and the Great Commission. We desire to mobilize millions of such leaders who, by the power of the Holy Spirit, will establish, nurture and multiply biblical churches and faith communities.

Third, we can *promote and practice partnerships* in the body of Christ. Since its inception in 1951, Campus Crusade has been instrumental in bringing individuals, churches and mission organizations together in powerful partnerships. Much of GCM's work will be to stimulate partnerships and participate in networks with others who share a similar vision, so that together we can accomplish what one organization or church could not do alone. We realize that it will take kingdom perspective, generosity and intentional effort to facilitate partnerships that will enhance the unity of the church, as well as good stewardship and strategic coordination of resources.

Fourth, we can *support and initiate church-multiplication movements*. In addition to pioneering evangelism, discipleship and church planting in areas where there are no or few churches, we can support others who are involved in the Great Commission. We offer our support in any way possible to existing churches that are seeking renewal or are working toward church multiplication.

Fifth, we can *develop and share tools, strategies and resources*. God has blessed our organization with many creative strategies, tools and processes — such as the MC2 (Multiplying Churches and Communities) training process and the various products of the Jesus Film Project. We have willingly given these away to others to use. And we plan to continue developing new and relevant tools, strategies and methods.

Another significant outcome from that first meeting in South Africa was to craft a simple description of the type of church we desire to see planted and multiplied. Accordingly, we agreed that the church or faith community needs to have 10 or more followers of Jesus Christ who share the characteristics of the early church as described in Acts 2:42-47: regular gatherings for prayer, worship, Bible teaching and fellowship; Holy Spirit-empowered obedience to the Word of God; a commitment to actively draw people to Christ in word and deed; and the presence of recognized spiritual leadership able to sustain and multiply the communities of Christ.

Building My New Team

In addition to learning from one another and developing a common global framework, my third objective through the consultation in South Africa was to recruit a few people to join me and my wife, Shewa. As people got engaged in group work, I carefully observed the contribution of every individual.

Eventually, I invited Jeanne-Marie Theron, Virgil and Kathy Anderson, and Jim Whelchel to join our team, as well as Lui Whelchel, who had not been at the meeting. The Andersons attracted me as strategic thinkers who are also gifted in measurements and reporting. A few months after joining my team, Virgil pioneered the development of a mapping and measurement tool that we now call *iShare*.

I was impressed with the Whelchels because of their experience working with Christ's Commission Fellowship, a megachurch in Manila, Philippines, that specializes in multiplication of discipleship groups. The Whelchels also served as professors at the International Graduate School of Leadership in Manila, where Jim helped develop and launch a practical leadership training for pastors. I eventually asked Jim to lead a task force that would develop our training and coaching curriculum.

Jeanne-Marie, my administrative assistant, played a vital role in helping me accomplish all that God had given me to do, and I invited her to continue to do so as I moved into a new role.

Questions for personal and group reflection

1. What are some of your highlights from this chapter?

2. Have you experienced the diversity of the body of Christ in your community by visiting different churches?

3. Has your own ministry fully defined its mission statement and core contributions to the body of Christ?

4. Please respond: *One step I will take to implement what I've read in this chapter is* _____

_____

_____

_____

The first Global Church Movements consultation in Pretoria, South Africa, May 2010

CHAPTER 14

Five Million Churches

"I will build my church, and the gates of Hades will not overcome it" – Jesus (Matthew 16:18)

Four months after the initial consultation, I had our first planning meeting with my new GCM team — seven of us — in eastern Pretoria in September 2010. There, God impressed upon our hearts a grand vision to help establish an additional 5 million churches and faith communities worldwide.

With a marker in my hand and a flipchart in front of me, I facilitated the meeting, asking a few questions that the Lord used to birth the vision.

First, I asked, "What do the words of the Bible in John 3:16 mean to us?"

It is one of my favorite verses, summarizing the entire Bible in only 26 words: "For God so loved the world that he gave his one and only Son, that whoever believes in him shall not perish but have eternal life."

Love motivated the Father God to send his Son, Jesus, to be crucified on the cross so that we could be forgiven and saved from our sins. By taking the initiative to mercifully deal with our sins, God offers unconditional love to the whole world, to every man and woman from every color and creed.

There are two destinies, and every person has to make a choice: Believing in Jesus leads to eternal life, while rejecting him leads to eternal condemnation.

Then my second question: "How many people live in the world?"

By September 2010, the global population was nearly 7 billion, though by the time of this writing it has grown to nearly 7.9 billion.[73] These are not just numbers, but unique individuals created, known and loved by God. Can you imagine a team of seven ordinary people planning to take the whole world for Jesus? Were we crazy? Not at all. God's plan has always been for the whole world — every person, tribe, tongue, people and nation.

My next question to the team: "How many of these people claim to be Christians?"

We looked at the global statistics. Irrespective of the level of understanding of the Scriptures and commitment to follow Jesus, about 2 billion people claimed to be Christians,[74] while the remaining 5 billion people did not identify themselves with Christ. Many of the latter have never even heard his name.

In that room, we came face-to-face with two giants. The first giant: how to help the 2 billion Christians grow in their commitment to follow Jesus and obey his Great Commission. The second giant: how to share the love of God with the 5 billion people who did not yet understand God's eternal plan and unconditional love for them.

And how would we know when the gospel had been made available to all the people in the world?

That's when I felt prompted by the Holy Spirit to suggest to my team: "It's when we have a church or a community of disciples of Jesus among every 1,000 people on planet Earth."

That means, if we had a church, a faith community or a group of disciples — actively witnessing for Jesus in word and deed — in every rural village, suburban neighborhood, urban high-rise, digital space, and in and through every relational network, then we could say the gospel had gone to every tribe, tongue, people and nation.

For a tiny team of dreamers in that small boardroom in Pretoria, the possibilities suddenly seemed extraordinarily probable. We fixed our eyes on what I had written on the flip chart. We trusted that God would use us to help:

- mobilize the 2 billion Christians to fulfill the Great Commission
- engage the 5 billion people with the gospel of Jesus
- plant a vital church among every 1,000 people everywhere
- see an aggregate of 5 million additional churches planted

Virgil Anderson interrupted our thoughts. "This is a holy moment," he said. "Let's go on our knees and dedicate this vision to God." We fell on our knees, praised our loving Father for the privilege of serving his purpose in our generation, and surrendered ourselves and the vision to him.

Taking the good news of Jesus to 5 billion people and planting an additional 5 million churches would not be too much to ask of God. For God said, "Ask me, and I will make the nations your inheritance, the ends of the earth your possession."[75]

If the body of Christ were able to love one another, embrace a common global goal, coordinate resources and work together, nothing would be impossible to achieve — because God is able to fulfill what he asks us to do.

The vision of planting 5 million additional churches and faith communities was never going to be a goal for one organization but the commitment of all those who value the kingdom of God and embrace the prayers of Jesus in John 17. When we received that unprecedented vision from the Lord in September 2010, we did not know how we were going to fulfill it, but we trusted God for his guidance and agreed to start casting the vision by faith.

Our Move to America

I had accepted my new global role, formed my initial team, and started working on the vision and strategies of the new department. But the idea of relocating to America was a tough one for my family.[76] Through previous relocations from Ethiopia to Zimbabwe, and then from Zimbabwe to South Africa, we had lost meaningful relationships with families and friends. Our children, especially, suffered this pain. Now this would be our third international relocation in about

10 years. We were also concerned about the social and spiritual environment in America for our children. Shewa and I prayed for God's wisdom and direction.

To avoid the challenges of another relocation, I asked Steve Douglass if I could do my new role from either South Africa or Ethiopia. With Steve's positive response, I started working from South Africa. Nevertheless, after attempting to do so for a few months, I realized the implications on my team and the work. With all the other Campus Crusade vice presidents based in Orlando, Florida, I was missing the informal and face-to-face interactions.

So we made the decision to move. After securing a work permit; selling, giving away or shipping our possessions; and handing over my role to my successor, Farai Katsande, our family of six left Johannesburg in January 2011. Three new team members recruited just a few weeks earlier — Jerry and Grace Sharpless and Dan Willmann — met us at Orlando International Airport and welcomed us to America.

Jerry and Grace had been on staff for more than 40 years, with rich experiences of serving internationally in East Asia as well as handling various leadership responsibilities. I asked Jerry to lead the operations of our department. He and Grace also became our cultural guides to the U.S., helping us to learn our new environment.

Dan Willmann, who had become one of my closest friends since we met 10 years earlier, was a gifted fundraiser for the Jesus Film Project. He joined my team as director of development. However, eight months later he was recruited away from my team to the position of global vice president for fund development. Jim Whelchel led our global field strategies. Virgil Anderson gave leadership to measurements. With our core leadership team in place and confirmed regional GCM leaders, we began aggressively casting vision.

On the family front, Shewa and I were not sure we would be able to raise adequate financial support, since most African Christians who support missionaries tend to stop their giving when the missionaries move to countries with better economies. But we believed that God who had called us would also provide, so we prayed.

We had already witnessed God's faithfulness through our previous relocations. For example, when we moved from Ethiopia to Zimbabwe, we had needed to raise almost three times more finances, and God provided. And when we moved from Zimbabwe to South Africa, we again needed to raise more, and again God provided.

Indeed, God has always prepared partners who took care of our needs. We were never alone and lacked nothing. When we arrived in Orlando, one of our generous ministry partners provided temporary housing for the two months before moving to our own house. More than 10 years after that move, Shewa and I are still grateful to God and to our partners who have stood alongside us in their prayers and financial support.

Also, contrary to the fears we had for the spiritual life of our children in America, all of them have been baptized since we moved to the U.S. God has been faithful to care for us in every need and concern.

Saying Goodbye

Five days after landing in America, we received news from Ethiopia that my father had passed away. He was an evangelist, elder, mentor, leader and prayer warrior who helped so many people reconcile with God and with one another. A faithful soldier of Jesus for nearly four decades, he inspired me and many others to follow Christ wholeheartedly.

I had visited my father about two months before his death, when he gave me a kiss and prayed for me. Leaning on his stick and walking slowly, he escorted me to the car and waved his frail hands. I did not know that it would be the last kiss, the last prayer, the last escort and the last goodbye. I thank God for my parents, who were role models of love, faith, prayer and perseverance. I have learned from my father about the power of the gospel in transforming a life, the power of hope in enduring hardship, and the power of prayer and faith in experiencing God and his many miracles.

My father didn't live for himself but for his family and for others. To meet our daily needs for food, he had traveled to far places searching for jobs. Though illiterate, he made education a priority for his children. He proclaimed the gospel of Jesus with grace and power — casting out demons, healing the sick and leading many people into the kingdom. He had such a big impact on people that about 6,000 people attended his funeral.

As his life story was written and read by the elders of his church, I heard one story about my father that was new to me. A year or two before we became believers in the Lord — back when I was 3 or 4 years old — God had appeared to my father in a brilliant light and said, "This light will change your life and will go out to the whole world from your family."

From where I stand now, in a global ministry, I see God's promise to my father in that small village in Ethiopia being fulfilled.

A History Course on Global Christianity

In 2011, while my family and I were settling in the U.S., I took a course on the history of global Christianity from Bakke Graduate University. I had already been in full-time Christian work for nearly two decades, but I knew little about the past struggles and triumphs of Christianity, nor the sacrifices made by many as they developed, defended and transmitted theology.

The books I was required to read helped me realize not only the greatness of God's grace but also the smallness of me. That awareness arose in me one morning during the course when I walked through a valley of lush vegetation and towering trees near the Canadian border. As I gazed upon magnificent mountains radiating the rays of a glorious sunrise, I felt full of gratitude to God for his creative genius and unconditional generosity.

Along with 16 students from various countries, I studied God's kingdom on earth through his church over the last 2,000 years. Dr. Ray Bakke unpacked the riches of God's grace using the Book of Matthew, focusing on the genealogy of Jesus. He described Matthew's intentions of including four women in the genealogy of Jesus — women who were foreigners, gentiles and with undesirable backgrounds like me — to show us that Jesus came from all, and for all, humanity.

Dr. Bakke also offered a compelling overview of Christian history over the last 20 centuries by taking us through "The Mission Trail at Bakken" — an artistic display of 20 saints who have shaped his theology and spirituality.

Each student was then asked to identify 20 saints who have influenced his or her own worldview, considering four distinct eras: Early Church (30-590), Medieval (590-1500), Reformation (1500-1648) and Modern (1648 to present). My list included individuals who taught me the value of vision, courage, commitment and sacrifice, such as:

- Tertullian of Carthage (160-225) — the concept of the Trinity

- Athanasius of Alexandria (296-373) — a life of simplicity and service

- Frumentius of Ethiopia (300-380) — the first bishop of Ethiopia

- Augustine of Hippo (354-430) — Christian theology, validity of Scriptures, origin of evil

- Yared of Ethiopia (505-571) — father of the culture of music and worship of the Ethiopian Orthodox Tewahedo Church

- Estifanos of Ethiopia (1380-1450) — initiator of the Ethiopian Church Reformation, martyr

- Onesimus of Ethiopia (1856-1931) — former slave, first evangelical convert in Ethiopia through the Swedish Evangelical Mission, reformer, and translator of hymns and Scriptures into the Oromo language

- Bill Bright of America (1921-2003) — co-founder of Campus Crusade for Christ who inspired me to believe God for the impossible

On the Shoulders of Giants

Christian history is the history of God's grace and unconditional love and the story of these spiritual giants whom God has chosen to fulfill his purpose on earth. As the students presented their 20 saints, I was amazed that, with few exceptions, each of us listed different heroes. We chose people connected to our respective identity, calling and mission — those who made significant impressions, influenced our voices and continue to inspire us.

We are the product of history and the fruit of faith, prayer, pain and suffering of many godly men and women. And then our gracious Father invites us to be a paragraph in the eternal book of his kingdom — the book that is being written by the blood of the Lamb and the toil and tears of saints. We are never alone.

Dr. Bakke taught us that history is not a telephone directory of the past but an opportunity for us to actively engage with that past — to contextualize what we learn with the aim of preserving what is good and resisting what is evil. Too often, human beings fail to learn from history, repeating the mistakes while thinking that they are the only ones making history.

As we continued to unravel the riches of Christian history in that course, we observed that the saints who have gone before us leveled the rough ground, so that we may walk on smoother paths. They were not perfect. Indeed, God accomplishes his glorious and eternal purpose through men and women who are weak, sinful and mortal. Yet despite their weaknesses, these saints faithfully fought internal and external forces so as to proclaim, preserve and defend the church of Jesus Christ. Through their travails, they shaped the landscape of Christian theology, worldview and practice.

The issues they grappled with included heresies and internal divisions, power and greed, theological and philosophical differences, persecutions, human philosophy and wisdom that contradicted God's wisdom, problems related to incorrect interpretation and application of the Bible, lack of human freedom and equality, and the dichotomies of faith and work, secular and sacred, and state and church.

Through that class I learned that I am a product of God's grace, the environment around me and the influence of many people. As Sir Isaac Newton expressed, "If I have seen further, it is by standing upon the shoulders of giants."[77]

Just as countless people, including Tertullian, Augustine, William Carey and others on my list, have shaped my worldview and Christian spirituality, I would also like to influence as many people as possible in my generation.

The course gave me a fresh sense of conviction and passion to promote ecclesiastical unity. Of course, there are differences in cultural, traditional and doctrinal expressions; but all Christian churches are united in the conviction that Jesus Christ is Lord and in the essential tenets of Christian faith, which fourth-century theologians and church fathers incorporated in the Nicene Creed.[78]

Hence as I serve God's purpose in my generation, my role will never be to divide but to unite the church, foster the centrality of Christ and his cross, and focus on what is essential and common to all: the eternal kingdom of God.

Multiplying Churches and Communities (MC2) Training

After our team ensured a worldwide consensus on GCM's ministry framework, we emphasized that different regions and nations should contextualize it. Next, we wanted to develop a relevant and transferable training process to help implement the vision. To do this, Jim Whelchel set up a global team of experts and practitioners.

The team studied the Book of Acts, the essential principles and core materials of our own organization, and the best training materials available in like-minded churches and agencies. The lessons learned shaped the outcome of GCM's training process, which we called "Multiplying Churches and Communities" or MC2.[79]

MC2 equips church planters to develop and multiply sustainable church movements, thus ensuring that the congregation they plant goes on to continue planting healthy churches that plant other healthy churches.

The process enables a person to know how to:

- engage a given geographic area, people group or community through evangelism and church planting
- apply the principles of a "Person of Peace" or a "House of Peace" as well as "Prayer-Care-Share"[80]
- start and disciple a group or a church
- immediately mobilize new believers for ministry

- raise up new leaders for multiplication
- grow and lead a healthy church

Since its development in 2011, MC2 has been field-tested and evaluated in various regions of the world. As a result, the process has been refined several times, resulting in the third version of MC2, which has three overlapping yet distinct pathways: Launch, Multiply and Develop.

The *Launch* pathway enables church planters to know how to engage a given community with the gospel and start new discipleship groups. Through the *Multiply* pathway, church planters engage in discipleship and church multiplication. As they continue to lead their new groups and churches, the trainees go through leadership development using a *Develop* pathway.

The effective application of the three pathways ensures in-depth discipleship and focused leadership development while at the same time leading to rapid multiplication of disciples, groups and churches. Moreover, MC2 employs adult education techniques such as reflective learning and practical application. It is an outcome-based training that discourages people from attending additional training without applying what they have already learned.

Since 2011, more than 120 countries have implemented MC2, with encouraging results. In some countries we have seen rapid multiplication of churches up to 10, 15 or even 25 generations. Some of the keys to sustaining such rapid growth include immediate mobilization of new believers for ministry, leadership development, effective coaching processes and emphasis on multiplication.

A Paradigm Shift

In launching Global Church Movements, we affirmed that God had called Campus Crusade for Christ to be a catalyst in church-multiplication movements, but not a church denomination. Moreover, our staff members are not necessarily called to serve as pastors of local churches. Rather, they serve as apostolic leaders who inspire, equip, coach and serve.

With the decision to start a global church-planting division, our organization also made strategic shifts from some of the ways we did ministry in the past.[81] Those shifts include moving away from:

- counting gospel exposures and indicated decisions through the showing of the "JESUS" film . . . to using the film to plant churches

- doing random evangelism . . . to building relationships with Persons of Peace and Houses of Peace in communities that need church planting

- forming temporary discipleship groups . . . to building movements of sustainable and multiplying churches and faith communities

- resourcing churches and other mission agencies with tools and training . . . to partnering with them around shared vision and optimized contributions

To create a better understanding of those shifts and to explain the GCM framework as a church-planting division of Campus Crusade, we recruited and trained staff members while organizing vision-casting conferences around the world.

Jesus is building his church all over the world. His light is penetrating the darkest places in the world and his kingdom is growing. We are witnessing that nothing is too hard for God. We must believe God for the impossible and take tangible steps of faith toward what he has called us to do. Then we will experience God and his mighty power.

In all this, we are never alone. The Creator of the universe is with us. We are not laying the foundation but continuing to build on the one laid by Jesus and the apostles. We should never make the mistake of thinking we are writing history, for we are only contributing to the history God is writing through the tears, toil, and blood of countless men and women who follow and serve him wholeheartedly.

Questions for personal and group reflection

1. When have you or your ministry dreamed for something too big for you to accomplish alone?

2. Bekele's team aimed to see a church or community of disciples planted among every group of 1,000 people on the planet. What's the biggest dream on your heart right now?

3. What have you learned from the processes Bekele and his teams followed to initiate, develop and expand Global Church Movements?

4. Please respond: *The five saints who have most influenced my worldview are:* _____
   _____
   _____
   _____

Bekele's father holding a shepherd's staff

CHAPTER 15

Learning from Others

"I pray . . . that all of them may be one,
Father, just as you are in me and I am in you"
— Jesus (John 17:20-21)

T he writers of the four Gospels — Matthew, Mark, Luke and John — stated
that Jesus prayed many times. But they only included the content of his
prayers a few times. Chapter 17 of John's Gospel marks the longest and probably
the last prayer of Jesus before his arrest. There, Jesus poured out his heart to his
Father, interceding for the unity of his disciples and for all who would believe
in his name.

> "My prayer is not for them [*his original disciples*] alone. I pray also
> for those who will believe in me through their message, that all of
> them may be one, Father, just as you are in me and I am in you. May
> they also be in us so that the world may believe that you have sent
> me. I have given them the glory that you gave me, that they may be
> one as we are one — I in them and you in me — so that they may
> be brought to complete unity. Then the world will know that you
> sent me and have loved them even as you have loved me."[82]

Since Campus Crusade was new at church planting, we organized vision trips
for key leaders and sent them to learn from other like-minded organizations.
We learned from writers and practitioners of church-planting movements such

as David Garrison, David Watson, Steve Smith, Ying Kai, Steve Addison, Curtis Sergeant, Ed Stetzer and Jeff Sundell. And we took time to learn from many organizations, including The Timothy Initiative, Dynamic Church Planting International, Christ's Commission Fellowship, Faith Comes By Hearing and Northland Church.

The Timothy Initiative

In the summer of 2010, I had met David Nelms, founder and president of The Timothy Initiative. I have yet to meet a person as passionate for Jesus and the Great Commission. As senior pastor of Grace Fellowship Church in West Palm Beach, Florida, David felt the Lord's leading to start a church-planting ministry. About three years before our organization started a church-planting department, David established TTI.

TTI implements a simple church-planting strategy: recruiting and training people who are like the apostle Paul, who then recruit and train people who are like Timothy, who then recruit and train people who are like Titus. Every trainee is challenged to start a church within a year of starting the training and to raise up new leaders.

With his contagious love for Jesus, tremendous energy and dedication to church planting, David is a spiritual giant. When you hear the name TTI and the amazing work they do all over the world, you may think TTI is a large organization. That is not true, but what makes TTI big is the big heart David has for the Lord Jesus and for his church. I don't know how he does it, but David is everywhere and does everything. He is not only president of TTI but also an evangelist, fundraiser, trainer, speaker, organizer, partner and world traveler.

After learning about TTI's strategies and visiting their church-planting work in Kenya, we decided to partner with them in six countries in Africa. As we observed, we realized they had compelling vision, solid commitment and absolute integrity but lacked adequate financial resources. At the same time, my department in our organization had about $400,000. So my team and I decided to give half of that money, so that they could plant more churches. In turn, God kept bringing more resources to us. God is a giver, and he is delighted when we give to others.

Why did we give away the money that belonged to our organization? Haven't our donors entrusted that money to us? Did we compromise our integrity? We gave the money because we maintained a kingdom perspective — one of the cultural elements in our organization. The churches planted through TTI belong to the Lord. Our donors would also be happy to know that we were leveraging the resources for the highest possible return on investment.

Sharing resources generously with those who build the kingdom of God has always been part of our organization. And the results of that investment were extraordinary: over 1,500 churches planted in six countries in just 18 months.

Dynamic Church Planting International

Another organization that contributed to our initial learning process was DCPI, founded in 1994 by Paul Becker, a former staff member of our organization. During the first half of 2011, Paul visited our office in Orlando. Jerry Sharpless and I shared with him details about our newly established church-planting department and our vision of helping to plant 5 million additional churches worldwide.

I saw tears in Paul's eyes. "It has taken God 23 years to answer my prayer," he explained. "I have been praying for God to speak to your leaders to start planting churches and consolidate the results of evangelism that Campus Crusade for Christ is known for. Now I thank God for this new day in the life of your organization."

A few months after Paul's visit to Orlando, Jerry and I visited the DCPI office in San Diego. We learned that when Paul and his team started the organization, they had set a goal of planting 1,000 churches by the year 2020. However, by the time we visited in 2011, DCPI had already trained about 50,000 people, who may have contributed as many as 85,000 new churches in about 90 countries. Yet their vision was even larger than that. "The Lord increased our goal in 1997 to 1 million churches and in 2009 to 5 million churches," Paul told us.

There it was again: 5 million churches. God was obviously conveying a huge vision for church planting to others in the body of Christ. And it continued.

Joel Hunter, then senior pastor of Northland Church in Orlando, had asked his congregation to believe God for 1 million distributed churches.[83] Church leaders in the Philippines were dreaming about training 1 million Filipino tent-makers as church planters. Pastor Peter Tan Chi, founder and senior pastor of CCF in Manila, Philippines, had a vision to plant 200,000 churches. And e3 Partners had a goal of planting 1 million churches.

God was calling many of us at the same time to dream big, so big that God alone could accomplish it.

Before Jerry and I left San Diego, we agreed to partner with DCPI in selected countries.

Faith Comes By Hearing

Whenever we visited any organization, we had three major objectives: know the leaders, learn from them and find ways to partner. In August 2011, Jerry Sharpless and I visited the Faith Comes By Hearing headquarters in Albuquerque, New Mexico, and met the organization's president, Morgan Jackson.

The ministry was established in 1972. At the time of our visit, FCBH had 125 staff at its global office and a few regional leaders around the world. In relation to organizational infrastructure and staff size, they were smaller than our organization. But in terms of fulfilling their specific area of calling, they were bigger. They had set a goal to translate and provide audio Bibles in over 2,000 languages and establish Bible-listening groups, implementing most of their work through partnerships.

By the time we visited, FCBH had already made audio Scriptures available in about 1,000 languages spoken by 6 billion people in more than 185 countries. While seated in their state-of-the art media room, Jerry and I witnessed live streaming of Scriptures being downloaded and uploaded in various languages all over the world. The Word of God was penetrating the darkest corners of the globe. FCBH also provided "Proclaimers" — digital audio players prerecorded with Scripture, often a New Testament. A Proclaimer is an effective tool for both evangelism and discipleship.

After agreeing to enhance our existing partnership, Jerry and I left Albuquerque feeling inspired. Since then, Faith Comes By Hearing has added great value to the work of our organization and improved the quality of our discipleship process. They gather new believers in Bible-listening groups, especially after showings of the "JESUS" film. In turn, our organization, with infrastructure in nearly 200 countries, can help expand their work globally.

God has already provided all the necessary tools, strategies and resources to the body of Christ to complete the Great Commission. We need each other.

Christ's Commission Fellowship

Peter Tan Chi, senior pastor of CCF, began an evangelistic Bible study in 1982 with three couples in Manila, Philippines. Today it has grown into a global movement. As those three couples invited their friends, the initial group grew to transform the lives of businessmen and women, professionals and families, who in turn have become leaders in the church's amazing multiplication network of "Dgroups" (discipleship groups).

Inspired by the church's model of these discipleship groups and of business CEOs serving as full-time pastors, I couldn't find a better place to take a large delegation of GCM leaders from across the world. So as we sought to establish ourselves, I took our leaders to visit CCF for three consecutive years — 2010, 2011 and 2012 — and immerse themselves in its ministry.

We sat and watched Peter Tan Chi facilitate his own Dgroup.[84] The members had stayed in the same group for more than 20 years and had built a solid relationship. We witnessed the power of sharing life together in a small community of like-minded men. Far more than a simple Bible study, the members know each other intimately, care for one another deeply and take the Great Commission seriously.

Moreover, each member of the group was leading his own Dgroup, the members of which were in turn leading their own Dgroups — developing multiple generations of disciples. As a result, CCF has become one of the most powerful movements of discipleship and church-planting in the world, a megachurch impacting the globe. When people who have experienced Dgroups in CCF relocate to other parts of the world, they take the vision and principles of multiplication with them and start churches in the image of CCF.

By the time of this writing, CCF has more than 80,000 members in the Philippines, has planted over 33,000 churches and faith communities around the world, and has built a massive infrastructure in metro Manila as a center for worship and leadership development. The church raised the entire $80 million needed to build the center from within, and without debt.

From Strength to Strength

By the end of 2012, we'd introduced the MC2 training process worldwide, gleaned best practices from multiple other organizations, and organized vision and training conferences attended by 371 leaders from 108 countries.

We then produced a third edition of the GCM framework in 2013 — reflecting our commitment to continually assess our tools and processes. We also emphasized collaborating with other ministry strategies within our own organization, which is diverse and complex.[85] Such intentional collaboration would enable us to optimize resources and increase impact.

Fast-forward to the end of 2020, and we were thrilled to report:

- GCM established in 152 countries

- 2,600 GCM staff and 117,000 associates providing leadership to church-planting within our own organization

- 73,000 church planters engaged in our training process (just in 2020 alone)

- at least two generations of church multiplication in 117 countries

- 182,000 churches and missional communities established since GCM's launch in 2010

Jesus never promised his church a smooth ride in this broken world. But he told us the church will be persecuted as he himself was persecuted, and the gates of hell will wage war against his church. However, we know who will win. The church of Jesus is a victorious church and the gates of hell will not overcome it. Through the grace of God and the passionate commitment of men and women of God to proclaim Jesus in word and deed, GCM has continued to grow from strength to strength.

Questions for personal and group reflection

1. What captivated your heart the most in this chapter and why?

2. Why do you believe partnering is critical in the body of Christ?

3. In what ways has your own church or ministry shared valuable resources with another without expectation of repayment?

4. Please respond: *I will take steps this week to start a new ministry partnership (or expand an existing one) with* _____

_____

_____

_____

CHAPTER 16

Better Together

"A cord of three strands is not quickly broken"
(Ecclesiastes 4:12)

One day back in 2011, I had been praying and thinking about the vastness of the world and the enormity of the work we needed to do, to plant a church or faith community for every 1,000 people. At that moment, I felt the Holy Spirit remind me, "You are not the only one serving my purpose. Your organization is not the only one involved in the Great Commission. Go and work with others."

Of course! As GCM we were already partnering with many likeminded organizations, but could we align further?

So in September 2011, even while encouraging the exciting growth of GCM, my team brought together about 15 leaders from seven organizations to talk about a cohesive alliance. At the meeting, Joel Hunter of Northland Church shared a short message from the Word of God, emphasizing, "God is more concerned about the alliance of our hearts than our institutions."

Leaders then presented highlights of their work and told stories of bold vision, faithful implementation and unprecedented opportunities for the gospel. Every leader spoke with humility and emphasized the priority of the kingdom of God above their organizations. They were willing to share with one another whatever resources God had given them. "It's not about me, it's not about my institution," they said. "It's all about God and his kingdom."

Indeed, in line with Pastor Hunter's devotional message, God created an alliance of our hearts so that we could create an alliance of our organizations. By 3 p.m., we had agreed to promote the kingdom of God in response to Jesus' prayer in John 17 and to work together for the glory of God. Steve Douglass concluded the meeting in prayer, committing us and the initiative to the Lord. God started something big on that day.

Five organizations would become the founding members of what we now call GACX, or the Global Alliance for Church Multiplication: The Timothy Initiative, Dynamic Church Planting International, Global Church Movements, Christ's Commission Fellowship and Northland Church.

The agreement to work together included sharing lessons learned, identifying priority locations and partnering in them, attending one another's strategic events, measuring toward our common goal of helping plant 5 million additional churches, and inviting other like-minded leaders to join us.

We didn't have all the next steps clearly outlined by the end of the meeting, but we made a commitment to have a shared vision, support one another and work together for the glory of God.

The Development of the Alliance

We held a number of follow-up meetings, one of which involved coming up with a working definition of *church*. We spent almost a whole day studying a 25-page paper on the identity, mission and function of the church. As a result, we wrote and agreed to use the following description:

> "A local church is a body of believers and followers of Jesus Christ, with recognized spiritual leadership, who regularly gather for worship, fellowship, instruction, the practice of the ordinances and sacraments, and who fulfill the Great Commission by loving and serving one another and their neighbors and intentionally multiplying themselves."

At another follow-up meeting, we identified critical next steps, including inviting others to join the alliance, setting the objectives and frequencies of future GACX forums, and agreeing to launch, practice, document and communicate the outcomes of our collaboration.

And then we got to work. GCM and TTI launched partnerships in Tanzania, Democratic Republic of Congo, Ghana, Nigeria, Burkina Faso and Niger — planting 351 churches in 10 months. GCM and DCPI agreed to partner in Botswana, Lesotho and Mozambique.

Paul Becker of DCPI, in one of his regular newsletters, expressed his joy of partnering:

> "There are some crucial actions we Christians do TOGETHER. Back in the 1700s, the Moravian missionaries had a motto: *'Together we pray. Together we labor. Together we suffer. Together we rejoice.'* This is what we do TOGETHER with others who share our vision. We pray. We work. We suffer. We rejoice. There is strength and love and encouragement for all of us in doing these things TOGETHER with one another and with God. What a privilege! What a joy! To do our part in the Great Commission TOGETHER with others."

In 2012, Erick Schenkel became the new executive director of the Jesus Film Project. He had previously planted and pastored a church in Boston before becoming a missionary in Central Asia, so he understood the role the "JESUS" film could play in accelerating church-planting movements. Therefore, he oriented the Jesus Film Project toward planting a church for every 1,000 people and made their tools available for local churches, mission agencies and church denominations.

GCM and Northland Church partnered in a number of countries before the church needed to scale back its vision due to internal changes, including Joel Hunter's retirement as senior pastor.

Meanwhile, GCM partnered with CCF in multiple countries. Jim Whelchel had been an important leader on my team, but when Peter Tan Chi asked for help, we seconded Jim to serve CCF as its full-time mission pastor. As the writer of GCM's training process (MC2), master strategist and practitioner, Jim helped take CCF's global church planting to a higher level. He pioneered and guided the planting of more than 15,000 churches in South and East Asia in about eight years.

To educate existing and potential members of GACX on the values, processes, practices and benefits of partnerships, we communicated stories of collaboration. Soon, other organizations began to join us in the alliance.

From 2012 to 2014, GACX membership grew from the original five organizations to about 30, including mission agencies such as e3 Partners and Every Home for Christ, and also Converge (one of the largest church denominations in the U.S.). We continued to inspire, challenge, support and learn from one another.

At twice-annual GACX forums, like-minded leaders connected with each other and were inspired by the growing impact of the kingdom. They spent time evaluating and refining existing partnerships and initiating new ones — all to leverage their resources and increase the quality and scope of their work.

After the sixth forum, we changed the frequency from twice a year to once a year. From 2014 to 2019, GACX membership grew to more than 80 organizations, and forum attendance expanded to more than 300 leaders representing more than 150 organizations.

GACX is an alliance of diverse organizations who value unified Christian witness, collaboration across diversity, and effective coordination of gifts and resources for optimum kingdom impact. Churches and organizations that are planting churches come together through GACX, as well as those that specialize in creating tools, developing leaders, mobilizing prayer and doing humanitarian work. They are not necessarily asking, "What can I get out of my GACX membership?" Instead, their primary motivation is to do whatever it takes — both giving and receiving — to help further the kingdom of God.

Moreover, GACX members share similar convictions. As long as Jesus is proclaimed as Lord and King, we value, respect and affirm any church size, expression, tradition and ministry methodology. We are better and stronger together. We are committed to sharing what God has given us because we believe that God's kingdom is bigger than any one of us. We also know that we can do nothing without the power of God. Therefore, we pray and mobilize others to pray, and take steps of faith toward accomplishing our common goal.

Local churches, mission organizations, church denominations and networks can be members of GACX as long as they:

- embrace the vision and the values of the alliance as described in its framework

- work in multiple nations or diverse cultures

- agree to measure, share and celebrate ministry progress with member organizations

- commit to planting directly or through partnerships at least 1,000 churches and faith communities (applies only to those who are planting churches)

- make an annual investment of at least $1,000 to help facilitate the continuous development and implementation of GACX's vision

International Expansion

As we continued to develop GACX, we became aware that although many of our member organizations were working in the same region or country, local teams didn't know each other. And in most places, national churches and indigenous mission organizations were not fully aware of the work of some of the global organizations in their countries.

To address these and related needs, we started initiating regional and national alliances. We brought together national teams of GACX member organizations and leaders of national churches and local mission agencies, so that they could know and learn from one another.

In some places, national leaders understood for the first time that abundant resources such as ministry tools, training processes, best practices and leadership development opportunities were available within their own countries.

They became aware of who is doing what and where, and agreed to set common national goals.

Within the last few years, we have seen the concept and practices of GACX expand globally, expressed as regional partnerships and national alliances. A few of these are listed below.

East Africa

In March 2015, 123 leaders representing Kenya, Tanzania, Uganda, Rwanda, Ethiopia, Zimbabwe, Democratic Republic of Congo and South Africa attended the launching of GACX East Africa in Nairobi, Kenya. Everyone left the conference committed to launch their own national alliances. (GACX had already been launched in Ethiopia the previous year, as our first international event.)

For example, leaders in Tanzania set a goal of planting a church in every city neighborhood and rural village: an estimated 67,500 churches. As a result, Tanzania has become one of the best examples of collaboration, aggressive church planting, rapid multiplication of disciples and churches, and church-based community transformation programs. As I write this, Tanzania has seen up to 26 generations of church multiplication within the past three years, due to newly planted churches planting churches that are planting churches.

Europe

The European forum for church multiplication launched in February 2017 in Barcelona, Spain. A total of 158 leaders attended, with about 30 percent of participants under age 35. Steve Addison, Australian author and researcher of Christian movements, reminded the European Christians of God's heart for the nations, the role Europe has played in global evangelization, and the power and practices of multiplication. The second European forum was held in Krakow, Poland, in 2018.

Taiwan

More than 100 leaders attended the launch in Taipei in August 2017, with a steering committee comprising leaders from the Fellowship of Mennonite Churches in

Taiwan, United Missions of Taiwan, Chinese Christian Evangelical Association and the Taiwanese Baptist Association. They agreed to pursue a vision of planting a church or faith community for every 1,000 people. By the time of this printing, Taiwan had completed five annual GACX forums.

Philippines

In September 2017, about 100 leaders attended a partnership event in Cebu, with another 100 attending a second one in Manila. In Manila, Bishop Noel Pantoja, leader of the Evangelical Alliance of the Philippines, spoke on the rapid growth of the church in his country and how they had identified about 23,000 villages, or *barangays,* without churches. Working together, they hope to see every *barangay* with a vital church.

Latin America and the Caribbean

In September 2017 in Guayaquil, Ecuador, 35 leaders representing 16 organizations and eight countries attended the first forum. They signed what they called The Guayaquil Commitment, agreeing to help plant one community of faith for every 1,000 people: "Let not one city, village, town, ethnic or digital community be without the presence of at least one community of faith."

Ten of the 16 organizations agreed to become founding members of GACX in the region. Since then, they have organized forums in Rio de Janeiro, Brazil, in 2018 and Mexico City in 2019, and the alliance has continued to grow.

Chad

About 450 leaders showed up in the capital city of N'djamena in December 2017 for the launch of the national alliance. During my opening remarks, the Holy Spirit prompted me to ask the participants to greet at least one person from another church denomination and declare, "We are one in Christ!"

I didn't have any information on the history and current affairs of the church in the country. But at that moment, God started healing a conflict that had existed in the Chadian church for about 46 years. Later, I was told that many groups had unsuccessfully attempted to reconcile the churches over the years. Two days into the conference, I had dinner with the presidents of 22 denominations and spoke on unity. Afterward, one leader said, "I like what you are saying. But we cannot work together because we are deeply divided and wounded. How can you help us?"

While I was praying for God's wisdom, I saw another leader standing up and walking toward the brother who had asked the question. Kneeling before the man, he grabbed his feet and said, "My brother, I am the problem in our country. Please, would you forgive me?"

After that initial response, the Holy Spirit took control of the room. As I prayed with those two brothers, another leader stood up and walked to another person, asking for forgiveness. I asked someone else to pray for those two brothers. And so it continued, with small groups of confession and prayer occurring all across the room. The dining room of a hotel became a holy ground.

As we concluded our unplanned revival meeting, I asked the leaders to preach in each other's churches and announce to the conference participants the next morning what God had done in their midst.

The next day, the entire group wept as we declared, "We are one in Christ. We have reconciled. We reject division. We commit ourselves to working together for the glory of God."

Pastor Manitha, who had witnessed the reconciliation at the dinner fellowship, gave a moving testimony. "I am 68 years old," he said. "I have asked God for a very long time that I might see the church in Chad unified before he takes me home. Last night, after the forgiveness and reconciliation, I told the Lord, 'It is enough. Now I am ready to go home.'"

As he administered Holy Communion for the group, Pastor Bimba Josue, chairman of Christian Assembly in Chad, called forward a leader of another denomination, embraced him and told the audience, "My brother and I have reconciled last night. We are one."

God wanted the leaders to stand on the foundation of love and unity, so that they could proclaim Christ together. After the reconciliation, the Chadian church leaders signed a document, agreeing to work together to plant over 5,000 churches and engage every unengaged and unreached people group in the country with the gospel.

Representatives from every French-speaking African country as well as Angola had also attended the conference. Many committed themselves to organize alliances, including Togo and Burundi, who launched in 2019.

Henri Ye, president of national reconciliation and unity in Burkina Faso, told me, "We have 8,500 villages in my country. We have a plan to plant 4,000 churches. But after hearing your presentation on multiplication, I am convinced we must change our plan. I believe we can plant 14,000 churches because some of the villages are big and need more than one church."

A Virtual Forum

The year 2020 saw the world shut down by COVID-19, yet this opened the door for even greater expansion, as GACX sponsored a global virtual forum. Some 4,000 people from 130 countries participated, with representatives from 44 countries meeting to discuss launching a national expression of GACX in their countries.

Truly, we are becoming united and working together, as Jesus prayed in John 17. We see God's favor on our unity and the vision he has given us. GACX is growing in depth, scope and impact. By spring 2021, more than 100 organizations were collaborating globally and had helped plant about 2.1 million churches and faith communities worldwide — almost 42 percent of our collective goal.

We have many areas of shortcomings. But we are open to learn and grow. We continue to believe God for the impossible. With all his authority in heaven and on earth, God is with us. We are never alone.

Questions for personal and group reflection

1. Has your church or ministry ever partnered with another in a large event? If so, what were some of the challenges? The blessings?

2. How would you define "church"?

3. What struck you most about the "unplanned revival meeting" that occurred during the GACX launch in N'djamena, Chad?

4. Please respond: *One step I will take to implement what I've read in this chapter is* _____

   _____

   _____

   _____

The GACX Global Forum 2019 gathered 319 people from more than 140 organizations.

Bekele addresses the GACX 2019 Global Forum.

Bekele and Nate Vander Stelt (GACX executive vice president)
on stage at the GACX 2019 Global Forum

CHAPTER 17

A Journey to My Village

*"Who am I, Sovereign Lord, and what is
my family, that you have brought me this far?"
— King David (2 Samuel 7:18)*

With five objectives to accomplish in 10 days, I took a trip to Ethiopia in January 2018. Before leaving home, I prayed for God's favor, protection and good health. During those 10 days in Ethiopia, I wanted to:

- visit my mother, who had been sick for a few months

- speak at a prayer conference

- preach at my niece's wedding

- visit our church-planting work in the country

- teach at a national pastors conference

I come from a large and loving family. So when I arrived at Bole International Airport in Addis Ababa, 14 family members greeted me. Along with Colin Millar — a dear friend and prayer leader from the U.S. — and several staff members with the Great Commission Ministry of Ethiopia, we traveled to my place of birth on January 18. Seven years earlier on that same day, my father had passed away. Because of poor roads, a 150-mile journey turned into about five hours of driving.

When we entered my mother's home, I couldn't believe my eyes. Her health had significantly deteriorated since my last visit a month earlier, and she didn't even recognize me. After being at her bedside for a few hours and committing her and the situation to the Lord, Colin and I left for the prayer conference, to be held on Hambaricho Mountain the next day.

Meeting Our God on the Mountain

Hambaricho Mountain is an important landmark for people of my ethnic origin and can be seen for miles in every direction. As I mentioned in the first chapter, a dynasty of powerful witch doctors, viewed as gods themselves, lived on the hills of the mountain.

During times of drought, infertility or tribal conflict, thousands of people would travel to the mountain to consult the "god," known as Abba-Sarecho, whose family had reigned there for centuries. For 22 generations, the firstborn son of the previous god had assumed the throne. People would approach the mountain with singing, dancing and prayer, passing through one of 30 gates (locally known as *gochos*) in order to climb to Abba-Sarecho's compound.

My friend Dr. Desta Langana, founder of Hambaricho International Prayer and Missions Movement, had been organizing prayer conferences on this mountain for 20 years. This year, he had invited Colin and me to speak. The one-day event had always been held on the 19th of January — an important day on the calendar of the Ethiopian Orthodox Tewahedo Church, celebrating the baptism of Jesus (Epiphany).

Starting at 1 a.m., tens of thousands of people would hike and climb the mountain, which rises nearly 10,000 feet above sea level and is flat at the top. I climbed the mountain for the first time in my life and experienced the stunning 360-degree view. If it had not been for God's intervention to save my family from spiritual darkness when I was 5 years old, I would probably have come to this mountain to honor Abba-Sarecho. But on that day, I was there to honor Jesus and preach the gospel.

Nobody knew the exact number of people on the mountain that day, but the estimates ranged from 50,000 to 100,000. According to Dr. Langana, the largest attendance so far had been 200,000 people. These people, primarily from the Kambata tribe (of which I am a part), were praying for the whole world, beseeching God to do the same work of transformation that he had done among our own people.

Dr. Langana believes that more than 94 percent of the estimated 1 million Kambata are followers of Christ, with a vital church in every village. One such church thrives about 150 feet from my mother's house. Even when she became unable to walk to the church due to her illness, she could listen to the message through a loudspeaker mounted on the church roof.

Almost every child and adult in the community goes to church on Sundays. Many attend prayer meetings and Bible studies during weekdays. Apart from the material poverty that still exists, I wish every village in the world could be like this.

It was not only my first time to be on this mountain but also my first time to speak to the people of my origin, because more than 30 years earlier I had moved to the capital city for college. As I spoke at the conference, I highlighted the story of my life and the power of the gospel to transform lives.

As I looked at those thousands of young men and women in front of me, I remembered my own life growing up in one of those villages below the mountain. I hoped and prayed that God would touch the life of every person the way he had touched mine. He has raised me up from that small village where I used to tend cattle and given me a global platform to serve his glorious purpose.

I encouraged the conference participants to love and follow Jesus and to educate themselves as well as their families. I prayed that God would bless them both spiritually and materially. I asked God to raise up many godly leaders and global missionaries among them. It was a privilege to have Colin Millar with me, who also spoke and prayed for the people.

We left before the conference was over because we needed to drive back to Addis Ababa in time for me to speak at my niece's wedding the next day. After a tedious descent followed by a long drive, we arrived in the city physically exhausted but spiritually rejuvenated.

A day after the wedding, Colin and I traveled to southeast Ethiopia, bringing with us several national staff members from Ethiopia and a few visiting

American Christians. Several of these individuals were partners in ministry and had come to see the fruit of their prayer and financial investment, including Harry and Cici Scott.

The Scotts Tell Their Story

In summer 2015, Harry and Cici had attended their first Global Briefing Conference, which Cru organizes for ministry partners. At that point, the Scotts had been involved with Cru for almost 20 years — supporting various staff members and investing in several different ministries. I found their story to be a wonderful example of *Never Alone*.

At that 2015 conference, the Scotts told me, they heard amazing stories and statistics about how God was working. "We considered ourselves pretty informed," Harry explained," but we had no idea how quickly the gospel was spreading to unreached people around the world. God put it on our hearts to not be on the sidelines. He was calling us to be all-in."

So Harry and Cici began asking God what he wanted them to do, and praying about how to get their friends back home in Austin as excited as they were "about how God is on the move."

"Because this wasn't the kind of stuff we heard at church," Harry said.

As they prayed, God drew their hearts to the need for church planting. They wanted to invest deeply in one location where they might also develop personal connections. God seemed to lead them to Ethiopia, a country from which friends of theirs had adopted children. "That was key for us," Harry said, "because we knew that we wanted to do this with friends. As you know, everything's better when you're doing it with people you love and enjoy."

The next year, they hosted a dinner for friends in Austin and invited me and another staff member to talk about plans for church planting in Ethiopia and how everyone might get involved. The initial goal was to help plant 100 churches.

"That seemed like a big goal to us," Harry shared, "and we were praying that our family could contribute to 50 of those churches. At that dinner, one of our friends encouraged all of us to add a zero to what we were thinking of contributing.

And that's when things began to get a little out of hand. The Holy Spirit moved, and so we added a zero to our goal. The group committed to help plant 1,000 churches in Ethiopia."

The giving started that night and continued over several months. Then, in January 2018, the Scotts traveled to Ethiopia to see the ministry in action and report back to their Austin partners. There, they visited some of the new churches in a rural area south of Addis Ababa and met both church planters and those who coached them. One congregation met under a large tree, another in a farmer's small house; more than a few gathered in makeshift buildings and huts. "All were joyful and filled with the Spirit of God," Harry said.

"Living in Austin, with the pervasive indifference and sometimes outright hostility to anything about Jesus, it's easy to forget that many people eagerly receive the gospel."

The Scotts' visit to Ethiopia confirmed God's calling and the truth of Matthew 6:21: "For where your treasure is, there your heart will be also."

The Scotts say they've found joy in investing their time, money and prayers on behalf of the people of Ethiopia. "We have always been happy to give, so that people can know Jesus," Harry said, "but this effort has felt a bit different. It's so much bigger than us, and it's clear that it's God's doing, not ours."

Vital Churches

On that trip with the Scotts to Ethiopia, we visited seven rural churches over a period of two days. Some were just a few weeks old and others a few months. The sizes ranged from 15 to 50 believers. Until our church planters started working in the area, few of the villages had any known believers.

In every church, the believers worshipped God wholeheartedly, prayed earnestly and studied Scriptures diligently. The leaders, primarily young men and women, were full of faith and the Holy Spirit. It felt like we were back in the book of Acts: obedience to the Word of God, bold evangelism, supernatural miracles and God adding daily to their numbers.

In spite of socioeconomic hardships and various forms of persecution, the communities were witnessing the transforming power of the gospel. Many have been healed from their sicknesses and delivered from evil spirits. Many witch doctors and former persecutors have become obedient to the Word of God. An old lady told me she was blind, but now could see. "Jesus has healed me!" she exclaimed.

The new believers witnessed boldly and the churches were growing. In the past, these areas had been difficult to reach with the gospel, but not anymore.

During those two days, we saw almost everything we had hoped for. As the Scotts mentioned, believers gathered in homes, under trees and in rented houses. They were being persecuted for the sake of Christ. Leaders were being trained and sent to take the gospel to the communities beyond the mountains and across the rivers, planting churches where there were none.

Most of the believers worked on the farms during the day and gathered together by night for prayer, Bible teaching and worship. Some churches met three times a week for a minimum of two hours. They prayed for people to be saved from their sins, for healing from physical infirmities and for the church to grow. They also prayed for themselves, that they would be bold and faithful.

As we visited those churches, we spoke the Word of God and prayed with them. We listened to their stories and shared their food. We also led some curious young people to Jesus. At our last stop, while we were sharing the good news, a mob came with sticks and rocks, demanding that the church planter stop the meeting immediately. The church planter was calm and knew how to respond. We were safe, but it showed us a picture of the hostility faced by men and women of God around the world.

It's Worth It!

I believe we will hear millions of stories in heaven, and many of them could be from the villages of Ethiopia. But let me take you back to the Scotts, to hear from Harry more of their journey of obedience and sacrifice — not unlike that of many of our ministry partners:

Jesus saved me as an adult. As I slowly gave him areas of my life, I was prompted to start giving. I still vividly remember writing my first check to the church. For someone whose previous giving involved throwing a few bucks in the plate as guilt compelled, that first check was a significant amount of money. I was puffed up with pride, and I remember being offended that I did not get a thank-you note from the pastor.

Well, as God grew me, he grew my understanding that as Scripture tells us in Deuteronomy, all that I have is from him and all that I have is for him and his glory. I am simply "returning" to God a portion of what he has entrusted to me.

Years ago, I accepted an invitation to go to Florida for a weekend fundraising event for a Cru ministry called Priority Associates. The formal fundraising request was made Saturday night. I prayed faithfully and heard very clearly from the Holy Spirit. The number I heard was big for me. I wrestled with it, but ultimately, I wrote it down on my commitment card.

I went to my room that night and immediately started feeling regret or "donor's remorse," I called it. What was I thinking? I slept terribly, but the next day while on the plane, the Lord got ahold of me. The dialogue went something like this:

"Lord, what did I do?"

"Did you inquire of me?" I heard this clearly, though not audibly.

"Yes."

"Did you hear clearly from me?"

"Yes."

"Did you obey me?"

"Yes."

"Then the rest is up to me."

I felt immediate relief.

That was on a Sunday. In a matter of days, I received my commission on a real-estate deal that was almost exactly what I had committed at the event in Florida.

Cici and I shared how the Spirit moved at our first Ethiopia event and how we were encouraged to add a zero to our original goal. Well, here's the rest of the story: When I had broached the subject of changing our goal, Cici informed me that she needed to go to the restroom. When she returned, she asked how we would make our commitment if we added a zero.

I said that God would have to provide in an unforeseen way or that I would have to empty my retirement account. That night and for weeks afterward, I was praying and trusting God to do just that: provide in an unforeseen way. Well, the short version of the long story is that He did not provide in an unforeseen way, and I emptied my only retirement account.

The years since we made that radical financial commitment have been the hardest of my life. I have experienced a betrayal in business that took our most valuable asset, our largest source of income and the largest portion of our net worth.

I don't have a pretty bow to put on the end of a finished story, but here is what I can tell you: We have never once regretted making that commitment or emptying my retirement account.

While this has been the hardest season of our lives, it has been without a doubt the most meaningful and joy-filled — to see our life count for eternity in ways far beyond what we could ever dream or imagine. This has been the richest time of our marriage and family life, and I would not trade it for anything.

Let me be clear: We do pray from the Book of Joel that God will restore the fields that the locusts have eaten, but he certainly has no obligation to do that.

So, do I still struggle with money issues? Of course. I think it will be a limp that I carry for the rest of my earthly life. But I have learned that success is not having or making lots of money; success is simply being faithful to God. He has allowed me to do that as Cici's husband and as Claire and Meredith's dad and as an incredibly ordinary guy saying "yes" to what God calls me to.

Between the time we started partnering with Ethiopia (October 2016) and now, we have seen 3,080 churches planted in 16 generations — far surpassing our initial goal of 1,000.

My Mother's Legacy

We concluded our visits to the churches and returned to the city in time for the pastors conference, where we expected more than 450 to attend. On January 23, about an hour before my first session, a call came from my village that my mother had just passed away. I immediately asked God to give me peace and wisdom. After a quick consultation with our staff, the schedule was adjusted so that I could teach most of my sessions before leaving for the village in the afternoon. I had God's peace and was able to teach calmly. Then that afternoon, I left.

When we arrived home, my mother was no more. I remembered her usual greeting: "My son, welcome home!" The questions she used to ask rang in my mind: "How was your trip, my son?" or, "How is Shewa?" or, "When are you going to bring your children to see me? I hope I will not die without seeing them."

The house was filled with people from near and far, but my mother was not among them. "Our days on earth are but a shadow," Job says.[86] And that is why we need to pray like David, "Show me, Lord, my life's end and the number of my days; let me know how fleeting my life is;"[87] or like Moses, "Teach us to number our days, that we may gain a heart of wisdom."[88]

Every one of us is given time and opportunities to do something meaningful. We must live each day with a sense of purpose and urgency. That's how Harry and Cici have been living their lives. That's how Jesus lived his life. And that's how my mother lived her life. She did something beautiful with her life: She lived for God and for other people.

Apart from occasional visits, I had been away from my village for more than 30 years. So I interviewed several family members to learn more about my mother and wrote up her life story. In addition to reading it to the thousands of people present at her funeral, I also preached the gospel and shared some highlights of my life. I encouraged those who came to mourn with us to learn from my parents and give priority to educating their children.

True, the early years of her marriage before knowing Jesus had been difficult. As already mentioned, the worship of evil spirits and resulting curses ravaged not only our family but also the whole community. But after receiving salvation and hope in Jesus Christ, their marriage became a shining example of love, trust and faithfulness.

Our home, once a place of conflict and chaos, became a place where the hungry ate, the homeless sheltered and the motherless found a compassionate mother.

My mother was a natural leader, a wise counselor and a gifted organizer. She was consistent in prayer, firm in faith, bold in action. Through her five children (three boys and two girls), my mother enjoyed a legacy that included 25 grandchildren and six great-grandchildren, all followers of Jesus.

Now, both my parents are gone, and the void is deep. But I know where they are and look forward to seeing them with all the saints in the glorious kingdom of God.

Questions for personal and group reflection

1. In light of the brevity of life on earth, how are you living your life every day?

2. What did you glean from Harry and Cici's story?

3. Have you ever trusted God for a financial gift larger than you thought possible? If so, what did God do with your gift?

4. Please respond: *One step I will take toward living a life with no regrets is*

   _____

   _____

   _____

   _____

Bekele visits church planters in Ethiopia during a 2018 trip with ministry partners.

Bekele's mother, Ersule Melsebo

Bekele's parents

On a 2018 visit to his home village, Bekele enjoys seeing his siblings and their families.

Bekele visits the National Unity Park in Addis Ababa, Ethiopia.

EPILOGUE

I don't know why you decided to read this book. Maybe you have known me, heard about me or wanted to know what on earth connects a village in Ethiopia with global leadership. I am glad you have read it. I hope you have been inspired by a story of God's love and grace. Through that grace, I was given not only a new life but also destiny and purpose.

The work of God in my father's life, the many miracles I witnessed and the favor of God have given me a solid foundation to believe God for big things. I am never afraid of asking God for the impossible, because I know all things are possible with him.[89] I also carry a deep conviction that it is not a sin to believe God for the impossible.

God's redemptive purpose in my life, my partnership with uncountable men and women, my education and training, many of my family's challenging circumstances, and the short service I rendered to the Ethiopian government have significantly shaped my life.

Since writing my personal mission statement in 2004, I have maintained a habit of daily reflection and journaling that helps me evaluate the effectiveness of my life and make sure that I am not wavering from my calling. When I was 36, I was confronted with career conflicts and four competing priorities. Now, 15 years later, I find myself involved directly or indirectly in all those priorities.

Throughout, I have learned a great deal about partnerships, and they hold a fundamental place in all that I am and do. Without partnership, life itself is impossible. We exist because of others.

As far as what might come next in my life, I am ready and willing to do whatever God wants me to do. Wherever God sends me, he will go with me; and whatever he asks me to do, he will do it with and through me.

God has been with me from my days herding cattle as an Ethiopian villager to my role in global leadership. He is the link between the two extremes. He has always brought amazing people into my life: family members, friends, colleagues, partners, supervisors, teachers, mentors and so on. They have prayed with me, cried with me and sought to serve God's purpose with me. They have trusted me, invested in me and instructed me.

I have never been alone, nor will I ever be.

Nor will you.

APPENDIX A:
LEADERSHIP LESSONS

During my years of ministry around the world, I have learned valuable lessons that shaped how I lead. These include:

1. *Learn from those who have led in the past.*

    Take the necessary time to learn from previous leaders of your organization. Every leader is a part of history — linking the past, the present and the future. One of the greatest pitfalls for new leaders is the rush to introduce their own ideas before taking time to listen, understand and learn from people who have gone before (including those who currently serve in the organization).

2. *Be willing to dream big.*

    You've heard it said, "If you aim at nothing, you'll hit it every time." When you believe God for the impossible and take giant steps of faith, God shows up, and you find yourself empowered to accomplish great things for him. But when your plan is too small, there is no need for God, because you can do it yourself.

3. *Listen and ask good questions.*

    By inviting someone else to talk first about their dreams, plans and suggestions, you not only demonstrate humility but also lay the groundwork for productive discussions. Despite your level of experience, you can always learn from others.

4. *Never criticize others in the body of Christ.*

> Regardless of their traditions and practices, every church that calls on the name of the Lord Jesus is your church and deserves your love, respect and service. When we work together in the kingdom of God, we are stronger and more powerful.

5. *Don't be afraid to ask.*

> People are capable of generous giving. But they are often waiting for a bigger vision, a clear plan and a passionate ask — an assurance that contributions are making a difference in the world.

6. *Be willing to pursue unity*

> Fulfilling a large organizational vision requires strong internal unity, clear ownership and the unwavering commitment of all stakeholders. Invest the hard work upfront to make these a reality, and then you can run with the vision.

7. *Big vision and bold leadership attract people and resources.*

> People don't give their resources just because they hear a great plan but because they are moved by your convictions, see a clear path to follow and trust you to take them there.

8. *God's promises in the Bible are always true and he is faithful to fulfill them.*

> Live by these promises in all that you do, and trust in them for every bold step you take.

9. *Opposition makes you wiser and stronger, shapes your character and leads to a greater dependence on God.*

> Opposition will find you (you don't need to look for it), but God will carry you through.

APPENDIX B:
PARTNERSHIP PRINCIPLES

Partnerships hold untapped potential to unlock hidden resources, achieve common goals and bless everyone involved. Let me share some powerful principles I have uncovered over the years:

1. Most of the resources we need to do God's work are found not far from where the work needs to be done. The main problem is our inability to work together and match resources with needs.

2. The kingdom of God is bigger and more important than my local church or organization. Key ingredients of true partnerships that further the kingdom of God include a bigger vision, a pure motive, a humble heart and a spirit of generosity.

3. True partnerships benefit all partners, not just one group.

4. With partnerships, we can expand our scope and increase our impact.

5. For partnerships to happen, somebody has to initiate.

6. Sacrificial giving is crucial to a successful partnership. In an environment where each partner is more concerned about *what to give* than *what to receive*, God ordains abundant blessing.

7. Partners are attracted to you because of your history, vision, passion, credibility and results. Therefore, it is important for you to keep your history right, your vision clear, your passion strong, your credibility intact and your results visible.

8. One organization's *critical needs* are another organization's *available resources.* Through strategic partnerships, these two elements are brought together and matched toward addressing common challenges.

9. Effective partnership starts with a shared vision and a common mission. Consider these pivotal questions whenever you invite others to join in your visionary plans:

   a. What do you think of the vision? *A question of conviction*, necessary to create ownership of the vision.

   b. How would you refine this vision? *A question of involvement*, necessary to give opportunities for leaders to shape the vision.

   c. What potential challenges do you anticipate? *A question of problem-solving*, necessary to prepare leaders to solve problems in their cities.

   d. What contributions can you and your organization make toward fulfilling this vision? *A question of commitment*, necessary to mobilize resources.

   e. What critical next steps would you take in your organization, city or country? *A question of action*, necessary to help leaders begin developing plans.

APPENDIX C:
PARTNERSHIP PROCESS

Follow this process to design, develop and implement partnerships:

1. Ask God for a big vision: You need partners only if your vision is too big for you and your organization alone.

2. Take the initiative: Partnership cannot happen in your office. Don't wait for people to come to you, but rather take the first steps to identify and meet potential partners and build relationships.

3. Find common needs and opportunities: Partnerships are based on solving common problems, seizing common opportunities and fulfilling common interests. So, identify those problems, opportunities and interests.

4. Agree to work together: Partnership truly begins when two parties agree to work together, not in adjacent lanes.

5. Develop a common vision: Effective partnership is all about fulfilling a common vision and practicing a shared leadership.

6. Bring the best contribution from each side: Identify what each partner can bring to the table (leadership, financial resources, strategies, experiences, influence, etc.).

7. Match needs and resources: Identify if you need to mobilize additional resources or postpone addressing some of the needs.

8. Develop a plan: A clear plan contains measurable goals, answering the questions who, what, when, where, why and how.

9. Start working together: Start small, implement, evaluate progress and learn from it.

10. Expand: Based on the lessons you have learned, expand your partnership as God leads.

APPENDIX D:
OPERATION SUNRISE
DECLARATION STATEMENT

(Made on June 30, 2001, at the Vision and Partnership Conference in Nairobi, Kenya)

Recognizing the greatness and sovereignty of God the Almighty and Creator of the universe,

Recognizing the love of God demonstrated to us by giving us His Son, our Lord Jesus Christ, whose death and resurrection provides for our salvation,

Recognizing that in His Word, Jesus Christ our Lord gave us the Great Commission to go into the entire world and preach the gospel and make disciples of all nations,

Recognizing the moral, spiritual, social, political, and environmental wounds of our cities and nations,

Recognizing the promises of His inspired Word, particularly as declared in Malachi 4:2, "But for you, who revere my name, the sun of righteousness will rise with healing in its wings. And you will go out and leap like calves released from the stall."

It seems good to us, delegates gathered in Nairobi, on this day of June 30, 2001, and the Holy Spirit to affirm the initiative of Operation Sunrise Africa — to reach out with the gospel of our Lord Jesus Christ to the

50 million, living in 50 cities of the Southern and Eastern Africa (SEA) region in 50 days.

We the body of Christ, in realization of the fulfillment of the Operation Sunrise vision and the significant role of Africa in the world, in the preservation and promotion of biblical Christian values, individually and collectively resolve to humbly stand together in unity to:

Mobilize believers for concerted prayer.

Mobilize the body of Christ to lead in promotion of justice, peace and reconciliation.

Mobilize human, financial, material and other resources.

Mobilize strategic partnership.

Creatively spread the gospel of Jesus Christ using all ethically appropriate means.

ACKNOWLEDGMENTS

Many people have been involved in the stories and the writing process of this book. It would not be possible to list all of them. I deeply appreciate my wife, Shewalem, and our children Nathan, Elim, Philip and Nesiel. Thank you for understanding the cost of writing and allowing me to spend significant time away from you. Thank you to staff members in our organization, friends, colleagues, and ministry partners in Ethiopia, Southern and Eastern Africa, and around the world for your role in my life and ministry. This book is possible because of you.

To you, my friends, teachers, mentors and partners Ramesh Richard, Jimmy Seibert, Steve Douglass, Dick Eastman, Rick Warren, Aklilu Dalelo, Michael Whyte, David Nelms, Teketel Yohannes, Grace Barnes, Tessema Ersumo, Ray Bakke, Dale Hummel, Stephanie Hayes, Girma Bekele, Scott Ridout, Nate Vander Stelt, Dela Adadevoh, Roy Peterson and William S. Wojcik — I am deeply indebted that you took your precious time to read the manuscript and give me invaluable input and endorsement. Thank you to Pastor Dale Hummel and the Wooddale Church in Minnesota for your generous support.

My special appreciation to you, Stefan Dell, for giving leadership to the entire project; Rachel Postler, my former administrative assistant, for wisely navigating through my heavy schedule and creating time and space for me to focus on writing; Bill Sundstrom for editing the draft manuscript and guiding the publishing process; Diane McDougall for her careful attention to the final manuscript; family members and friends for encouraging me to write the stories of God's work in my life; men and women around the world for laboring with me in serving the purposes of God in our generation; friends and partners who gave me permission to share stories of partnerships in this book; and BookBaby for publishing this book.

Finally, I am grateful to God, my Creator and Redeemer, for his unmerited grace since my childhood and for enabling me to complete this project.

ENDNOTES

Chapter 1 (My Redemption Story)

1   In Isaiah 61:1-3, the prophet Isaiah predicts the mission of Jesus and the impact of the gospel. Then in Luke 4:18-20, Jesus declares himself the fulfillment of the prophecy.

2   Isaiah 9:2.

3   Bekele's father had already divorced his first wife after all her children died and she had returned to live with her family.

4   John 10:10

5   Abba-Sarecho was not happy at this, of course, and he tried to put curses on Bekele's father and the village. But God protected his new followers, and the curses had no effect. Many years later, Abba-Sarecho finally surrendered his life to Christ.

6   2 Timothy 4:7.

7   Genesis 2:18.

Chapter 2 (My Formative Years)

8   Before Eritrea became an independent country in 1993, Asmara — now its capital — was the second-most-important city in Ethiopia.

9   Isaiah 49:16.

10 Says Bekele, "I am forever grateful to God for sending that student, Teketel Yohannes, to talk to me about Jesus." At the time of this writing, Teketel is president of the largest evangelical denomination of Ethiopia (Kale Heywet Church) and a distinguished professor and scientist at Addis Ababa University.

11 Known as Cru in the United States.

12 When Bekele was in grade 9, 43 of his high-school teachers were taken to a valley and brutally executed by the communist government, then thrown into a mass grave. Courses such as math and physics were abandoned during the final three months of the semester because so many teachers were gone, and grades from the first semester were simply copied to report cards for the second semester. Hundreds of thousands of other innocent Ethiopians were massacred because they didn't agree with the political direction of the country.

13 Ethiopia's communist regime lasted from 1974 to 1991. In a 1988 interview with the *Los Angeles Times*, Berhanu Bayeh, then Ethiopia's foreign minister, acknowledged an increase in church attendance but added that the regime had "a duty to show them [that] all this mystification of religion is absurd. . . . Through education they will realize they are mistaken."

14 Proverbs 18:22.

15 Watchman Nee, *Do All to the Glory of God* (New York: Christian Fellowship Publishers, Inc., 1974), p. 24.

16 "These friends included Yenenesh Zenebe, Eleni Yacob, Aster Kiros, Aklilu Dallelo and Tegene Legesse," says Bekele, "who played important roles in the early stages of our relationship as what I might call 'peer mentors.'"

Chapter 3 (My Early Ministry)

17 The "JESUS" film is a two-hour presentation based on the Gospel of Luke and translated into 1,900 languages as of May 2021.

Chapter 4 (Partnerships: Untapped Potential)

18 Bekele's team challenged business leaders to redeem the wedding rings so that they could give them back to the owners. And since the ministry had collected lots of gold, the ministry opened a gold shop in the office in 1998.

19 The new year is based on the Ethiopian calendar, which is a solar calendar that differs from the Gregorian calendar used in most countries. On leap years, the Ethiopian new year begins on September 12.

20 Luke 9:49-50.

Chapter 5 (Local Sustainability)

21 This simple way of outlining the primary points of the gospel begins: "Just as there are physical laws that govern the physical universe, so are there spiritual laws that govern your relationship with God."

Chapter 6 (Kingdom Financial Principles)

22 Acts 20:35.

23 Ecclesiastes 11:1 (New American Standard Bible).

24 Haggai 1:6.

25 Haggai 1:5.

26 Matthew 6:34.

27 Genesis 41.

28 Ethiopia's 1983-85 famine led to hundreds of thousands of deaths, according to the United Nations.

29 "Ethiopia Poverty Assessment 2014," The World Bank (Washington, D.C.: World Bank Group, 2015).

Chapter 7 (Operation Philip)

30 The love that Abebe and his wife, Berhan, had for each other was unusual. They always ate from the same plate and never let anyone sit between them.

Berhan was so devastated by the sudden and untimely death of her lover that she questioned God's wisdom and prayed for her husband to come back to life. She even challenged Bekele's faith and asked him to pray for Abebe's resurrection. Instead, Bekele encouraged her to trust in God's sovereignty. Rather than bring her husband back from heaven, God decided to take Berhan as well. One afternoon, while relaxing with her kids in a swimming pool, exactly 10 years to the day after her husband's accident, Berhan suddenly and peacefully passed away, leaving behind four children, now ranging from age 9 to 15. But God has been faithful to the children. He blessed each with talent, wisdom and opportunities. They passionately follow and serve God, and together they have founded a family enterprise in Ethiopia that specializes in film production and digital communication.

31 Acts 8:31.

32 In Luke 21, Jesus appreciated the sacrificial gift of the widow by saying that she had "put in more than all the others."

33 See Chapter 2 for details on how the government put pressure on the Christian fellowship at Addis Ababa University during this time.

34 Exodus 17:12-14.

35 Esther 3.

36 Genesis 1:2.

Chapter 8 (Operation Philip: Results)

37 Matthew 16:18 (New American Standard Bible).

38 John 17:20-23.

39 There was one final thing God did during Bekele's years leading the national ministry. Because of Ethiopia's inadequate road infrastructure, he had long wanted to buy two helicopters for the ministry so that they could fly to every remote village, show the "JESUS" film, train people and plant churches. They were in the process of buying their first helicopter from Switzerland when the government denied permission because Great Commission Ministry

was an "evangelistic organization." A year or two later, however, leaders from Helimission in Ethiopia (a medical mission) told Bekele that they had bought the same helicopter and brought it to Ethiopia, and that GCM could use it whenever they needed to.

Chapter 9 (Operation Sunrise Africa)

40 Jeff Desjardins, "Mapped: Visualizing the True Size of Africa," Visual Capitalist, Feb. 19, 2020. The article contains a graphic that compares the size of Africa to these other regions.

41 "The Largest Human-Made Lakes in the World," World Atlas, Copyright 2021.

42 Although occupied by Italy from 1935 to 1941, Ethiopia lays claim as the only sub-Saharan country to never have been colonized. So Bekele and his wife were unfamiliar with the idea of private property.

43 Tatenda Chitagu and Rick Noack, "Before Robert Mugabe was hated, he was loved," *The Washington Post*, Sept. 16, 2019.

44 Fortunately, as Bekele's immediate team got to know him better, most warmed up to him and the vision God was placing on his heart.

45 Oswald Chambers, *My Utmost for His Highest* (Uhrichsville, OH: Discovery House Books, 1992), p. 271 (devotional message for September 27).

46 Malachi 4:2.

47 Bill O'Donovan, *Biblical Christianity in Modern Africa* (UK: Paternoster Press, 1995), pp. 1-2.

48 Matthew 5:13-14.

49 D. Martin Lloyd-Jones, *The Cross: God's Way of Salvation* (Eastbourne: Kingsway Publications, 1986), xi.

50 Chambers, op. cit., p. 260.

51 Micah 6:8.

52 Other team members shared as well, presenting powerful examples tied to various task forces. Dickson Obwoya presented the prayer and church

mobilization task force; Timothy Mwangi handled the mobilization of students and development of creative strategies; Danny Lynch took care of strategies to reach professionals; Stanley Chege demonstrated how to organize executive outreach events; and Diana Langerock highlighted the use of various ministry materials and strategies.

53 See Appendix D for a copy of the Operation Sunrise Declaration Statement.

54 Mark 10:27; John 14:12-14; 1 John 5:14.

55 Haggai 2:8; Malachi 3:3; Romans 4:17-25 (NASB).

Chapter 10 (Operation Sunrise Africa: Results)

56 For example, Northland Church from Orlando, Florida, brought about 300 people to Windhoek, Namibia. Oak Pointe Church in Novi, Michigan, which had been partnering with the Great Commission Ministry in Zambia since 1998, mobilized its congregation for involvement in Zambia and beyond.

57 Malachi 3:3.

58 Bekele adds that the list of such generous financial partners included, but is not limited to, Bob and Shirley Shirock, Bill and Lynne Wojcik, Doug and Anne Williamson, Skip and Sharon Ast, John and Karen Harrison, George and Melodee Cook, Ed and Wendy Bjurstrom, Paul and Ruth Lindholm, Pierre and Sandra Tullier, Bruce and Sharon Chandler, and Ray Hood-Phillips.

59 Operation Sunrise response rates (selected cities):

Country	City	Number of people exposed to the gospel	Number of people indicated decision for Christ	Percentage of decision
Malawi	Zomba	19,573	9,920	50%
Lesotho	Maseru	51,814	25,930	50%
Tanzania	Mbeya	100,512	51,902	51%
Zambia	Lusaka	284,879	156,938	55%
Mozambique	Maputo	310,266	175,391	56%
Malawi	Lilongwe	161,444	93,967	58%
Swaziland	Manzini	9,780	6,846	70%
Zambia	Ndola	177,803	124,901	70%
Malawi	Blantyre	154,045	116,200	75%
Kenya	Eldoret	157,968	135,645	86%

Chapter 11 (Career Conflict)

60 From one of the posters in the Apartheid Museum in Johannesburg, South Africa.

61 "Professors such as Michael Whyte, former Azusa Pacific University provost, and Grace Barnes, former director of Operation Impact, continue to play a key role in my life and leadership," says Bekele, "and I deeply value their friendship, mentorship and partnership."

Chapter 12 (A 100-Year Vision for Ethiopia)

62 During Bekele and Shewa's move, God provided them with amazing people on both the African side and the American side to help both practically and financially during their time of need. From Africa: Dickson and Joy Obwoya along with their children; Jeanne-Marie Theron, Bekele's executive assistant; and other Campus Crusade leaders on the continent such as Danny and Margaret Lynch, Ken and Patty Borgert, Naton and Michelle Kamanga, Stefan and Marie Dell, Blackie and Noeline Swart; as well as real estate agents Dits and Dirk (a married couple in Pretoria). From the United States: the entire global leadership team, including Steve and Judy Douglass, and Dela and Elizabeth Adadevoh; as well as partners such as Bob and Shirley Shirock, Bill and Lynne Wojcik, and Paul and Ruth Lindholm.

63 Choosing what to sell and what to give away without his wife's consent, Bekele says, was one of the worst decisions he has ever made. "If you are a husband, please don't try that."

64 2 Corinthians 4:8-9.

65 Psalm 118:1,5,7.

66 James 1:27, Genesis 2:15, Matthew 5:13-16.

67 Luis Bush, "Ethiopia: The Move of God in Ethiopia," AD2000 and Beyond Movement, April 20, 1998.

68 Matthew 5:13-15.

69 Since that time, Bekele says, several aspects of the ENEC vision have been implemented through leaders who attended the congresses or were involved in the planning process. However, it became difficult to implement everything that had been intended in the original vision.

70 Matthew 28:20.

Chapter 13 (The Beautiful Body of Christ)

71 1 Corinthians 12:26.

72 The global leaders with Campus Crusade for Christ who participated in the 2010 consultation were Jim Whelchel and Wade Mantlo from the Philippines; Virgil and Kathy Anderson from Hungary; Markku Happonen from Germany; Guy Suffold from Canada; Geok Seng Lim from Malaysia; Bill Wolfe, Don Lovell and Bob Singleton from the U.S.; David Kim from South Korea; Allan Gibson from Australia; George Mamboleo from Kenya; Dickson Obwoya from Uganda; Jeanne-Marie Theron from South Africa; and Bekele from Ethiopia.

Chapter 14 (Five Million Churches)

73 2010 World Population Data Sheet, published by the Population Reference Bureau, July 23, 2010; and worldometers.org — a world population clock based on the latest estimates released in June 2019 by the United Nations.

74 "The Future of World Religions: Population Growth Projections, 2010-2050," Pew Research Center, April 2, 2015.

75 Psalm 2:8.

76 Indeed, Bekele's executive assistant, Jeanne-Marie Theron — a valuable member of the team up to that point — also eventually decided that she could not leave family behind in South Africa.

77 Sir Isaac Newton, in a letter to fellow scientist Robert Hooke in February 1675, as quoted at "BBC Learning English."

78 "The Nicene Creed: Where it came from and why it still matters," Zondervan Academic, March 9, 2018.

79 The MC2 training casts vision for how a church can multiply, teaches people to share their faith and testimony, and concludes by encouraging people to do a missional event reaching out to their network of relationships. Those that respond to the gospel can then enter a new missional community, which could either become a new church or a part of the wider ministry of the mother church. A second level of training for those who have established groups helps the new leader teach and disciple the new believers. In that training, the new leader takes believers through basic follow-up, then a two-year study of the life of Christ and the Book of Acts.

80 The term "Person of Peace" (similar to "House of Peace") refers to someone who displays openness to the gospel and to people of faith, whether or not he or she is a believer, and comes from Luke 10:6. The term "Prayer-Care-Share" illustrates a method of building relationships with those who don't yet know Christ: First pray for what concerns them; then show your care in tangible ways; and, finally, seek opportunities to explain how they can know Christ.

81 Since the start of the COVID-19 pandemic in 2020, GCM has made another strategic shift: from a historic emphasis on face-to-face ministry to an embracing of digital tools and strategies.

Chapter 15 (Learning from Others)

82 John 17:20-23. In John 17, Jesus also prayed for the protection of his followers and reported to his Father that he had fulfilled all he was sent to do.

83 Northland Church birthed its vision for "distributed churches" in 1998 — desiring that the church be "arranged around the relationships of the congregation and partner ministries, rather than around a physical building," according to its website. "Northland is calling people to follow Christ, distributing their lives every day in ministry to others."

84 If you have an opportunity to pass through Manila, consider visiting Christ's Commission Fellowship. Also include about an hour in your schedule to observe one of its Dgroups in action.

85 At the end of 1999, Campus Crusade for Christ had as many as 70 different ministries, reaching groups as varied as high-school students and business professionals, athletes and college students. Bekele believes they should collaborate for maximum impact. For example, every showing of the "JESUS" film can be used to start a church. Every high-school graduate coming out of a local church and going to college can be equipped to launch a new campus ministry or join an existing one. Every student who has been discipled on a college campus can become part of a church-planting movement.

Chapter 17 (A Journey to My Village)

86 Job 8:9.

87 Psalm 39:4.

88 Psalm 90:12.

Epilogue

89 Matthew 19:26.